Starmont Reader's Guide #61

Kurt Vonnegut

Donald E. Morse

Series Editor: Roger C. Schlobin

BORGO PRESS / WILDSIDE PRESS

www.wildsidepress.com

DONALD E MORSE, Professor of English and Rhetoric, Oakland University in Rochester, Michigan has taught, written about and lectured on the fantastic in literature and Kurt Vonnegut for many years. While Fulbright Professor of American Studies at Kossuth University in Hungary (1987-1989), he lectured at all the Hungarian universities with English Departments and at some of the Hungarian colleges on these subjects. In addition, he has twice given a series of lectures at Austrian universities (1985 and 1988), and once at several German universities (1989) under sponsorship of the USIA. In the United States he has given lectures or made presentations at professional meetings at over twenty states; abroad in addition to his Fulbright activities, he has lectured in France, Ireland, England, Yugoslavia, and Israel.

His publications include original satires and a short story; *The Fantastic in World Literature and the Arts* (1987), *The Choices of Fiction* (1974), and with Dr. Csilla Bertha, *The Green Rainbow: The Fantastic in Irish Literature and the Arts* (forthcoming); as well as articles on James Joyce, J. P. Donleavy, W. H. Auden, American Drama, the Teaching of English, Teaching Writing, the Teaching of Intelligence and Problem Solving, and the Fantastic and Postmodern Literature. With the Hungarian scholar, Csilla Bertha, he has translated several plays from Hungarian into English.

Besides his university teaching and research, he is a widely recognized Management Trainer and a licenced Trainer in Instrumental Enrichment—a program to teach thinking skills. For many years he has been the Conference Chair of the International Conference for the Fantastic in the Arts, served on the Board of Directors of the International Association for the Fantastic in the Arts, and edited the ICFIA conference papers for 1983. He has also been President, Vice-President, Director and Executive Secretary of the National College English Association. Currently he divides his time between the United States and Hungary.

CONTENTS

I. Chronology

This "Chronology" is based upon public sources including Vonnegut's writing and interviews, but is also indebted to Klinkowitz and Lawler, *Vonnegut in America* (3-6), and Giannone, *Vonnegut* (127-128).

1922   Born November 11 in Indianapolis, Indiana to Kurt, Sr., and Edith Lieber Vonnegut. Older brother, Bernard and older sister, Alice.

1940   Graduates from Shortridge High School, Indianapolis where he was one of the editors of its daily paper, the *Shortridge High Echo* during his junior and senior years.

1940   Enters Cornell University intending to major in biochemistry; columnist for the *Cornell Sun*.

1942   Spring: managing editor, of the *Cornell Sun*; fall: enlists in U.S. Army as an infantry private; sent to Carnegie Tech and the University of Tennessee to study mechanical engineering.

1944   Death by suicide of his mother. December 22, captured by Germans at the Battle of the Bulge; interned in Dresden, Germany.

1945   February 13, Allies bomb Dresden creating a firestorm in which 135,000 people die; May 22 repatriated; September 1, marries Jane Cox; December moves to Chicago, Illinois.

46-47   Works for Chicago City News Bureau as a reporter; graduate student in anthropology, University of Chicago.

1947   First child, a son, Mark born May 11. Moves to Schenectady, New York, where he works in public relations for The General Electric Corporation and its Research Laboratory.

1950   Publishes first story, "Report on the Barnhouse Effect," *Collier's* magazine, February 11.

1951	Leaves GE and moves his family to Provincetown, Massachusetts to write full time. Later moves to West Barnstable.
1952	Publishes his first novel, *Player Piano*.
1953	*Player Piano* published in London and chosen as a Doubleday Science Fiction Book Club selection.
54-56	Teaches English at Hopefield School for emotionally disturbed children; works for an advertising agency; opens second Saab automobile dealership in the United States.
1957	October 1, death of Kurt Vonnegut, Sr.
58-59	Death of sister, Alice, and brother-in-law; adopts three of their four children.
1959	Publishes *The Sirens of Titan* as a paperback original.
1961	Publishes *Canary in a Cat House* as a paperback original, his first collection of short stories. *The Sirens of Titan* reissued in hardback.
1962	Publishes *Mother Night* as a paperback original, although with a 1961 copyright date.
1963	Publishes *Cat's Cradle*.
1965	Publishes *God Bless You, Mr. Rosewater*; begins reviewing for the *New York Times Book Review*.
65-67	Teaches at the University of Iowa Writers [sic] Workshop.
66-67	Hardcover reissue of *Player Piano* and *Mother Night*; these and other novels reissued in paperback.
1967	Signs a three book contract with Seymore Lawrence, Publisher and Delacorte Press, who later reprint all his works in hardcover.
67-68	Receives a Guggenheim Fellowship; travels to Dresden.

1968   Publishes *Welcome to the Monkey House*, his second
        volume of short stories.

1969   Publishes *Slaughterhouse-Five.*

1970   Goes to Biafra to assist with shipments of food for the
        starving; receives literature award from the National
        Institute of Arts and Letters; teaches creative writing at
        Harvard.

70-71   October 7: *Happy Birthday, Wanda June* opens on Broad-
        way and runs until March 14, 1971.

1971   Publishes *Happy Birthday, Wanda June.* Receives M.A. in
        anthropology from the University of Chicago with *Cat's
        Cradle* as his thesis. Separates from wife whom he later
        divorces and moves to New York.

1972   March 13: "Between Time and Timbuktu," a ninety-minute
        special on public television; publishes *Between Time and
        Timbuktu or Prometheus-5*; son, Mark, suffers a schizo-
        phrenic breakdown. *Slaughterhouse-Five* produced as a
        film. Elected vice-president of the P.E.N. American Center.
        Elected to membership in the National Institute of Arts
        and Letters.

1973   Publishes *Breakfast of Champions* in a first edition of
        100,000 copies; chosen as main selection of three book
        clubs.

73-74   Fall, appointed Distinguished Professor of English Prose
        by the City University of New York; resigns in February.

1974   Publishes *Wampeters, Foma & Granfalloons*: a collection of
        reviews, essays, addresses and interviews from 1965-73.

1976   Publishes *Slapstick; Or, Lonesome No More* in a first
        edition of 150,000 copies.

1977   Birth of first grandchild, Zachary, son of Mark Vonnegut.

1979   Publishes *Jailbird.* Marries Jill Krementz, the photogra-
        pher, weekend of November 24-25.

1980   Publishes *Sun, Moon, Star* (with Ivan Chermayeff), a book for children.

1981   Publishes *Palm Sunday: An Autobiographical Collage*; a collection of personal reminiscences, interviews, reviews, addresses, occasional pieces, and letters by Vonnegut and members of his family.

1982   Publishes *Deadeye Dick*.

1985   Publishes *Galápagos*.

1987   Publishes *Bluebeard*.

II. Kurt Vonnegut:
"A Person from Indianapolis"

Almost alone among contemporary American writers, Kurt Vonnegut enjoys a remarkably wide readership: from young to old, popular to academic, and technologically sophisticated to naive. His work also serves an impressive range of purposes—social commentary, philosophical and theological discourse, ethical argument, parody, satire, prophecy. After three-and-a-half decades and a dozen published novels, he deserves to be acclaimed for what he is now and always has been: a pre-eminent American storyteller with a sharply critical, satiric vision whose major concerns as a writer and public figure include the great moral, social, and political issues of the mid-twentieth century—genocide, racism, the destruction of nature, first amendment rights, and the need for human community. It is also true of Vonnegut's work, as it is of the best writers and thinkers, that the whole is greater than the sum of its parts. When read together, his work forms a mosaic with a clear focus on the humanness of human beings, and the sacredness of life. "What is sacred to ... [Vonnegut]? ... Man... That's all. Just man" (CC, p. 143).

In October 1987, when Vonnegut published *Bluebeard*, his twelfth novel in thirty-five years, he listed fifteen of his other seventeen published books opposite the title page, to which he added this exclamation: "Enough! Enough!" In a less prolific, less tireless writer such an outburst might imply he was ready to call it quits, having reached the traditional retirement age of sixty-five, but with Vonnegut one never can be certain about such "traditional" actions. Earlier in *Breakfast of Champions*, he threatened to abandon novel-writing altogether in favor of play-wrighting, but since then, he has produced five more novels! (During this same fertile period, in addition to the books, he also wrote numerous uncollected stories, reviews, essays, speeches, and gave and rewrote several interviews.) His serious writing begins in 1952 with *Player Piano*, a satiric look at a future when automation takes over the world, leaving no room for human beings. From that beginning, Vonnegut moved through a series of

5

unforgettable, original creations in *The Sirens of Titan, Mother Night, Cat's Cradle,* and *God Bless You, Mr. Rosewater* to one of the best novels dealing with evil in the contemporary American experience, *Slaughterhouse-Five;* after which he wrote the comic masterpiece, *Breakfast of Champions,* returned to the fantastic in the "autobiographical" *Slapstick,* and the imaginative *Galápagos,* while also producing highly original works in *Deadeye Dick, Jailbird,* and *Bluebeard.* Of the other books, *Palm Sunday: An Autobiographical Collage* stands out as one of the most entertaining and revealing contemporary autobiographies by an American writer, using published pieces— such as speeches, reviews, letters, and other family writings—as opposed to private diaries. His play, *Happy Birthday, Wanda June,* despite its problematic ending, received remarkably good reviews, ran for a respectable five months in New York, and has since enjoyed many university and college productions.

Like the poet, W. H. Auden, who late in life turned to writing serious, light verse which, paradoxically, perhaps only a mature poet can do well, Vonnegut late in his career turned to writing serious, workmanlike fiction in *Deadeye Dick,* the story of a murderer; *Jailbird,* the confessions of one of the Watergate conspirators; and *Bluebeard,* the "hoax autobiography" of the Abstract Expressionist painter, Rabo Karabekian. What Auden wrote of Herman Melville applies equally well to late Vonnegut:

> Towards the end he sailed into an extraordinary mildness,
> And anchored in his home and reached his wife
> And rode within the harbor of her hand . . .

Kurt Vonnegut was born in 1922 in Indianapolis, Indiana, of German immigrant parents just in time to feel the crushing effects of the Great American Depression. For many children born during, immediately before, or right after the Great Depression, their own experience, as well as the scars the Depression left on their parents, often marked them for life. A friend of the family summed up the shift the Depression caused in the Vonnegut fortunes from very well-to-do—i.e., children in private schools and colleges, a large residence with plenty of servants, the ability to travel at will—to penury:

*(W. H. Auden, *Collected Poems,* ed. Edward Mendelson [New York: Random House, 1976], p. 200).

6

By the time K[urt] came along to his adolescence, the family was in financial trouble. He knew only the hard times of the 1930s. He was taken out of private school after the third grade, and sent to Public School No. 43 and then Shortridge High School [both in Indianapolis]. He was sent to Cornell University with specific instructions not to waste time or money on `frivolous' courses, but to give full attention to practical studies, principally physics and chemistry and math (PS, p. 54).

With Vonnegut, the Depression and its aftermath left its mark not only on his sensibility—he once characterized himself as "a child of the Great Depression" (PS, p. 117)— but also on his prose style, his sense of humor, and his values. As Jerome Klinkowitz says, "the great popular comedians of the American 1930s gave Vonnegut the basis for his artistic style, and his central beliefs can be seen as coming from an equally humble source: the lessons of his parents and schoolteachers from the same period."[1] His early experience also appears to have led him to appreciate the value of comedy as a paliative in life:

Comedians and jazz musicians have been more conforting and enlightening to me than preachers or politicians or philosophers or poets or painters or novelists of my time. Historians of the future, in my opinion, will congratulate us on very little other than our clowning and our jazz (PS, p. 140).

Like most men and women of his generation, "the last recognizable generation of full-time, life-time American novelists... [whom] the Great Depression... made... similarly edgy and watchful," the second major national and international event in his life was the Second World War, "which lined us up so nicely, whether we were men or women, whether we were ever in uniform or not" (PS, p. 1). In that war he was taken prisoner by the Germans during the Battle of the Bulge and had the extraordinary good fortune to survive the firebombing of Dresden as a prisoner of war. From *The Sirens of Titan* to *Bluebeard,* World War II is never far from the surface of his fiction, while in *Mother Night* and especially in *Slaughterhouse-Five* it lies at its very center. Other equally, if not more,

7

important events in Vonnegut's life occurred in his family and domestic life, including the deaths of his parents and sister, his marriage, his becoming the parent of three of his own and three adopted children, his eventual separation, divorce, and subsequent remarriage. Assessing the relative importance of these events, he says: "Being present at the destruction of Dresden has affected my character far less than the death of my mother, the adopting of my sister's children, the sudden realization that those children and my own were no longer dependent on me, the breakup of my marriage, and on and on" (PS, p. 301). While it is often difficult, if not impossible, to gauge the trauma of such events in another person's life, because Vonnegut is a writer, many of their consequences are observable in his works, and he has discussed many of them in interviews, essays, and the prefaces to his novels. These include his inability to write for a year after his father died; the difficulties and joys he experienced as a parent; his adopting three of his sister's four children "after" a series of horrendous events: "within a period of only twenty-four hours, their father drowned when his commuter train went off an open drawbridge in New Jersey and then their mother died of cancer in a hospital" (PS, p. 244). Later he was to remark: ". . . the most meaningful and often harrowing experiences which I . . . have experienced have had to do with the rearing of children" (PS, p. 156). Yet Vonnegut is clearly proud of all his children and delights in their various choices in life, and, in retrospect at least, looks with a certain pride at the notoriety they enjoyed growing up in West Barnstable, Massachusetts:

> they were such a formidable gang when they were young that one policeman became a specialist in their habits and haunts. . . .
> Nobody ever went to prison, though. Nobody ever dealt dope (PS, p. 249, and see also PS, pp. 244-54).

Of his separation and divorce Vonnegut is understandably discreet, yet surprisingly open. In interviews and essays he attempts to account for what happened, sometimes focussing on the shift in belief his first wife underwent that led her to practice a form of religion which he found intolerable (PS, pp. 192-218), and other times painfully aware of the phenonenon of two people once close growing further and further apart as the years pass until at last there is little or no communication between them:[2]

> Jane Cox Vonnegut and I, childhood sweethearts in Indianapolis, separated in 1970 after a marriage which by conventional measurements was said to have lasted twenty-five years. . . . we have been through some terrible, unavoidable accident that we are ill-equipped to understand. . . . we only just arrived on this planet and we were doing the best we could. We never saw what hit us (PS, p. 188).

Vonnegut once remarked in an interview with John Disney that "It does not hurt to be wounded. . . . it hurts afterward." If his separation and divorce was the "wound," then, clearly he hurt terribly afterwards and found he would receive neither support nor sympathy from his family. As only the second Vonnegut to get a divorce, he once remarked that: "More offensive to my relatives than my books, even . . . is the fact of my being divorced" (PS, p. 186). These strong feelings, which he sums up in the word, "embarrassed" or in the guilt-loaded phrase, "I await the police" (PS, p. 71, p. 191, and see also pp. 185-191), underlie, particularly, his writing in *Breakfast of Champions, Slapstick,* and *Deadeye Dick,* and his work in the theatre on *Happy Birthday, Wanda June,* which became part of his "running away from home" and his search for a viable community or "family" ("About This Play," WJ, n. pag.). Clearly Vonnegut took his own advice that he used to give to student writers; not only did he take it, but he followed it scrupulously:

> Find a subject you care about and which you in your heart feel others should care about. It is this genuine caring, and not your games with language, which will be the most compelling and seductive element in your style (PS, p. 77).

One of the attractions of Vonnegut's books is that most readers sense the depth of feeling underlying all the good fun and jokes and so become convinced that there exists a real Kurt Vonnegut behind them: a private human being with well-considered concerns, thoughts and feelings about himself, his work, world, and friends. Drawing upon his experience and feelings, he writes novels about subjects he

9

cares about with predominately two major themes: first, the difficulty or impossibility of coming to grips with the magnitude of evil experienced in the modern world, and second, the necessity for love and loving "whoever is around to be loved" (ST, p. 313). The context Vonnegut provides for exploring both themes is drawn directly from his experience of growing up in Indianapolis, leaving it for college and the armed forces, and then finding himself somehow unable to return:

> So—by the time the Great Depression and a Second World War were over, it was easy for my brother and my sister and me to wander away from Indianapolis.
> And, of all the relatives we left behind, not one could think of a reason why we should come home again.
> We didn't belong anywhere in particular any more. We were interchangeable parts in the American machine (SS, p. 7).

"We are so lonely," says Vonnegut in several interviews and talks, "because we don't have enough friends and relatives. Human beings are supposed to live in stable, like-minded, extended familes of fifty people or more" (PS, p. 180).

Thus Vonnegut's work reflects the incredible isolation contemporary Americans experience living in the highly mobile, atomistic society made familiar by both American literature and life. Tocqueville remarked on this phenomenon over a hundred-and-fifty years ago, when he wrote: "Democracy does not create strong attachments between men and men, but it does put their ordinary relations on an easier footing." What Vonnegut focusses on, however, is not the "ordinary relations" of everyday social or political life, but on "the unbelievability of life as it really is" (PS, p. 297) in those difficult times when a person needs the kind of "strong attachment" that offers understanding, warmth, and comfort to be "lonesome no more" (SS).

Because he cares about his subjects, his books have an immediacy that is often compelling, yet Vonnegut never preaches—not even in his most bitterly satiric novel, *Cat's Cradle,* which examines the human capacity for greed and duplicity that leads inevitably to the destruction of the world and which takes as pessimistic a view of humankind as the Latin satirist, Juvenal, did in his justly famous Tenth Satire, "On Prayer" or, in its most famous translation, "On the

10

Vanity of Human Wishes." Unlike Juvenal, Vonnegut never relies on invective and threat. Instead his chosen weapons are jokes, parody, playful invention, and, above all, the fiction of an objective narrator—all of which are far, far removed from Juvenal's lacerated world.

Given his reliance on humor and jokes—he once described his novels as "mosaics of jokes"—Vonnegut more closely resembles the other great Latin satirist, Horace, who attempted "to tell the truth laughing," and for whom there were, as Ronald Paulson says, "no real knave[s] in his world," but only fools.[3] Vonnegut also tells the truth through laughter and also sees most villains as simply fools, yet unlike much of Horace he does not rely on *savoir faire*, urbanity, and understatement while making use of false praise and irony. Nor are his moral and artistic values those of an urbane intellectual—such as Horace—whether of ancient Rome or contemporary New York but instead are those of an unsophisticated American pragmatist. His voice is that of the Middle West with its essentially conservative outlook and beliefs: "I myself find that I trust my own writing most, and others seem to trust it most, too," he writes, "when I sound like a person from Indianapolis, which is what I am" (PS, p. 79).[4] "Vonnegut's values," says Richard Giannone, "are those we associate with middleclass virtues. Decency, respect, neighborliness, success, and security are what his characters look for; and in the end, that commonplace search is rendered so tenderly that we can say that middle America also gave Vonnegut a moral scale."[5]

Nor, despite his focus on "the noblest study of mankind," is Vonnegut an American Alexander Pope believing in reason as the keystone of humanity's nature. From *Player Piano* to *Bluebeard*, human beings in his novels and stories appear motivated by every-thing *but* reason. In *Galápagos*, the narrator, from his perspective of a million years in the future, asserts that most of the problems on planet Earth have been caused by human beings having brains too big for their and everyone else's good; hence, evolution over the next million years will help the fittest, i.e., the small-brained, to survive. Whatever else they may be, human beings in Vonnegut's work are not portrayed as reasonable.

Rather than emphasizing a clearly defined view of the world based upon reason, such as that shared by most people during the Enlightenment, Vonnegut emphasizes the uncertainty contemporary

11

human beings experience from living in a random universe: "No respecter of evidence," he maintains, "has ever found the least clue as to what life is all about, and what people should do with it" (PS, p. 196). Nevertheless, he remains a moralist committed to humane values and perspectives who gives his readers a brilliant satiric portrait of his society and its negative values from World War II to the present. He does it not with Juvenalian invective and threat nor with Horacean laughter or Popean mock heroic deflation, but through carefully formed, often fantastic comic stories—a choice that places him in the company of such fantastic satirists as Lucian and Apulieus.

Lucian of Samosata, often credited with writing some of the earliest science-fiction stories, is generally acknowledged as one of the earliest fantasy writers who combined a marvelous literary invention with a fine comic sense and a keen satiric vision to criticize his society. In his most famous story, *Lucius, or The Ass*, he created an ideal narrator for his satire by adapting the folk tale of the man-in-an-ass's skin who becomes like the famous fly-on-the-wall: an invisible person before whom people will reveal their true values. Vonnegut in *Breakfast of Champions* invents a similar kind of narrator who behind his mirror-sunglasses not only observes, but also to a certain extent controls events and characters. As creator of his fictional universe, he can foretell the future and tell fortunes, including the most amazing of the most trivial events, such as who will succeed in obtaining radial tires for her car!—much as Swift earlier in the "Bickerstaff Papers" was also able to predict such exact, inconsequential happenings.

Apuleius, another of Vonnegut's literary ancestors, adapted, in his turn, Lucian's story for his delightful early novel, *The Golden Ass*. Apuleius gave the basic story of the man-transformed-into-an-ass an elaborate astrological and religious framework and used it to criticize his society from top to bottom. From the professions to the slaves, from the courts to the bandits, from the educated to the ignorant, everyone in the fantastic world of Apulieus is motivated by some form of greed: for money, sex or power, and no one escapes his satiric criticism. Similarly, Vonnegut satirizes people's greed for money, sex and power in *Cat's Cradle, Player Piano, The Sirens of Titan, God Bless You, Mr. Rosewater*, and *Jailbird*). Also in *Cat's Cradle* he uses the device of the fly-on-the-wall narrator in the person of the observing, uninvolved reporter writing a book on the day the world ended, together with the

12

founder of a new, modern religion to satirize the selfish, self-centered values that could lead to the destruction of the world: "'What Can a Thoughtful Man Hope for Mankind on Earth, Given the Experience of the Past Million Years?'... `Nothing.'" (*The Fourteenth Book of Bokonon,* in CC, p. 199).

In American literature, the satirical Mark Twain comes closest to being Vonnegut's literary foster father. Vonnegut named his firstborn son after him (PS, p. 172), paid him a writer's true compliment by using the conclusion of *A Connecticut Yankee in King Arthur's Court* as part of a contemporary war story in *Player Piano* (PP, p. 242), and built at least one of his novels, *Mother Night,* on Twain's exploration in *Huckleberry Finn* of the "tendency for . . . impersonators to get carried away by their impersonations, to become what they impersonate, and therefore to live in a world of illusion"—which exactly describes Howard Campbell as well as Tom Sawyer and Huck Finn.[6] Like Twain, Vonnegut is a moralist profoundly disturbed by the values of the society in which he finds himself; like Twain, he wrestles with the major moral and religious issues of his time; like Twain, he employs humor to deflate pomposity and destroy pretension; like Twain, and also Apulieus, he uses the fantastic in the service of his satire; and, finally, like Twain, in *Connecticut Yankee,* he despairs over humanity's inability to realize "what our planet could be," and its apparent willingness instead to settle for despoiling the Earth through war and the misuse of technology.[7] Vonnegut also criticizes the negative values he finds around him, values which Twain had earlier satirized, including greed; the lust for power; and the willingness, sometimes even eagerness, to destroy people and nature. Small wonder that Vonnegut repeatedly says he believes in the political importance of the arts.

To be convincing, however, a satirist, such as Vonnegut, must include in his work a set of positive values or a clearly articulated standard, against which the reader can measure the evil or the human shortcomings under satiric attack. In the first six novels, Vonnegut presents the values against which he asks readers to assess evil and waste: human beings miss their potential to be happy and to love in *Player Piano* by having nothing useful to do and so settling for inhuman work, in *Sirens of Titan* by engaging in meaningless relationships, in *Mother Night* by giving up their lives to an evil cause, and in *Cat's Cradle* and *Slaughterhouse-Five* by irresponsibly playing with the toys of death. This standard is most clear at the end of *The Sirens of Titan*, where Malachi Constant, after roaming the solar system for most of his life concludes that "... a purpose of human life, no matter who is controlling it, is to love whoever is around to be loved" (ST, p. 313). Similarly, in the preface to *Mother Night* Vonnegut says: "And yet another moral [for this novel] occurs to me now: Make love when you can. It's good for you" (MN, p. vii). Eliot Rosewater, the improbable hero of *God Bless You, Mr. Rosewater or Pearls Before Swine*, discovers the imperative to love "all creatures great and small" in a William Blake poem which he carefully paints on his stair risers:

> The Angel
> that presided
> o're my
> birth said,
> "Little creature,
> form'd of
> Joy & Mirth,
> Go love
> without the
> help of
> any Thing
> on Earth"
> (GB, p. 51).

Within these novels, this positive standard of holding, giving, sharing, and experiencing human love during good times and bad, during peace and war, remains constant, and against this standard all actions are measured. When the action is evil beyond comprehension, as in the Dresden massacre, where 135,000 unarmed civilians were incinerated almost overnight or in the Holocaust, where the Nazis attempted to annihilate the Jews, then, the novels understandably turn bittersweet. Lurking in the background and all around the edges of the pre-*Slaughterhouse-Five* novels are the unanswerable questions left over from World War II—the equivalent of a moral hangover. Questions such as How could people hate so unreservedly that they would attempt to annihilate another race or another group of people simply because they found them different from themselves? Why this terrible inhuman hatred that leads to massacres, to firestorms, to death camps, to atomic incineration? Why? As the main character in *Mother Night* says:

There are plenty of good reasons for fighting . . . but no good reason ever to hate without reservation, to imagine that God Almighty Himself hates with you, too. Where's evil? It's that large part of every man that wants to hate without limit, that wants to hate with God on its side. It's that part of every man that finds all kinds of ugliness so attractive.

It's that part of an imbecile . . . that punishes and vilifies and makes war gladly (MN, p. 190).

"Given such evil what is the purpose of history?" Vonnegut asks in *The Sirens of Titan* and *Cat's Cradle*. Both novels suggest, through their satiric views of the world, that all history is futile and void. What then is the purpose of life? Vonnegut has God Himself answer this question through the Bokononist creation myth in *Cat's Cradle*: "Everything must have a purpose?" God asks man. "Certainly," man replies. "Then," says God, "I leave it to you to think of one for all this...And he went away" (CC, p. 177).

In the pre-*Slaughterhouse-Five* novels, the bitterest satire occurs in *Cat's Cradle*, where the purpose of human beings, "to love whoever is around to love," is completely thwarted. On the day the world ended, the question, "Who is left for me to love?" becomes as meaningless as a bird's call at the end of a massacre, "*Poo-tee-weet*," and in its place is another terrible question: "How can I, in this now empty world, 'find some neat way to die, too'?" (CC, p. 190). Vonnegut, so clearly passionate about the sacredness of human life, comments trenchantly on human stupidity and folly. His view of humanity, however, culminates—at least in his fiction—not in continued bitter reproaches nor in invective and threat, but in the serenity of *Slaughterhouse-Five*—a serenity embodied in the Tralfamadorian total view of all time, which eventually the hero of the novel, Billy Pilgrim, is able to share.

Such serenity comes about, I believe, through Vonnegut's accepting the central place of suffering in human experience—suffering that may be as total as the firebombing of Dresden or the atomic bombing of Hiroshima. Donald Shriver, writing about Dietrich Bonhoeffer, the martyred Lutheran German pastor executed for his part in the plot to assassinate Hitler, says:

Suffering is the chief equalizer of human experience, and the authority of suffering . . . goes far on the way toward convincing us that there is such a thing as a "human community." Whatever the anthropologists tell us about human differences, a touch of suffering makes the whole world kin.[8]

What better place to assert the kinship of the "whole world" than when viewing it from Tralfamadore, a planet light years removed from all the petty squabbles here on Earth? But Vonnegut goes further, for he affirms the essential goodness of creation in Billy Pilgrim's epitaph: "Everything was beautiful and nothing hurt"—surely an appropriate epitaph for Billy or anyone else who is able to "come unstuck in time."[9]

But for the rest of humanity, as for later Vonnegut, the best hope lies not in coming "unstuck in time," but in living in time while employing the positive perspective found in Reinhold Neibuhr's prayer, which Montana Wildhack carries in a locket about her neck:

God grant me the serenity to accept the things I cannot change, the courage to change the things I can, and the wisdom always to tell the difference (SH, p. 181).

This prayer, familiar to many Americans as the prayer of Alcoholics Anonymous, describes the end point of the moral course of Vonnegut's first six novels as he moves from anger through disbelief to rebellion until he finally comes to accept what is and what must be. Behind this shift in vision, which influences his satiric viewpoint, lies Vonnegut's own acceptance of the mystery of human suffering and the presence of evil in the world for which there is not now nor can there ever be a fully satisfactory human explanation. Like Job before them, characters in Vonnegut's fiction ask, "Why me?" And like Job they hear only an echo, "Why not you?"

This acceptance enables Vonnegut in the novels after *Slaughterhouse-Five* to satirize particular evils in the modern world rather than wrestling with the question of evil itself. *Galápagos*, his eleventh novel, for example, makes brilliantly, satirically clear what many of his other novels, along with a Kilgore Trout short story "The Planet Gobblers" (PS, p. 209), had implied: human beings are a danger to the planet, and if they are not controlled in some way, they will destroy all forms of life. Alvin B. Kernan could have been describing the satire of *Galápagos*, when, over twenty-five years ago, he identified the object most frequently attacked by modern satirists as "an uncritical and simple belief in infinite progress, based on the improvement of

16

material conditions, on the development of science and on an ultraoptimistic assumption about human nature and its potentials."[10]

In other words, Vonnegut's fictional future—whether in *Galápagos* or *The Sirens of Titan, Slaughterhouse-Five* or *Player Piano*—reflects back upon the present, and is not only anti-utopian, but also runs counter to many of the themes and values found in some of the more traditional science fiction writing. According to James Gunn, science-fiction is rooted in the belief that through thinking humanity can indeed save the planet and itself; that through technology we will find a way out of the current ecological dilemma; that progress is not only possible, it is probable through science; and that finally "The farther into space one travels the less significant become the passions and agonies of man, and the only matter of importance in the long morning of man's struggle to survive is his survival so that his sons could be seeded among the stars."[11] To all of this Vonnegut says a resounding "No!" and from *Player Piano* and *The Sirens of Titan* to *Galápagos* and *Bluebeard* he continues to satirize such absence of value, neglect of the heart, and shift in focus away from the individual to the cosmos. Once, in response to a question John Disney asked him about whether he felt there was progress or if things were getting better, Vonnegut replied: "I don't have the feeling [that we are going somewhere]."

The acceptance of suffering as central to human experience, as well as that which helps define the human community, also helps account for the shift in those positive values against which he implies readers should measure his satiric attacks, for the emphasis in *Slapstick, Deadeye Dick, Jailbird, Galápagos,* and *Bluebeard* is on the necessity for establishing human community, for seeing "the whole world kin." In *Bluebeard*, his twelfth novel in thirty-five years, he satirizes the disastrous disassociation of head and heart and the distortion of values that occurs with the puffing up of a particular style of painting through excess wealth that, in turn, leads to all the problems associated with sudden fame and riches for obscure artists. (If Jay Gatsby had lived into the 1950s and collected art, instead of period rooms, then, he, too, would have a Karabekian on his wall in West Egg.) After wandering in the world of art as far as Malachi Constant did in the solar system, Rabo Karabekian returns home to the human community to celebrate life and—most miraculous of all—

17

to "love whoever is around to love," which in his case, as in that of so many of us, turns out to be himself (BB, p. 300).

The difference, therefore, between the early and late novels derives not so much from a major change in values or theme, as it does in a slight shift in attitude and tone. Vonnegut himself acknowledged this shift in his Commencement Address to the graduating class at Hobart and William Smith Colleges in 1974, where, somewhat bemused, he reflected: "For two-thirds of my life I have been a pessimist. I am astonished to find myself an optimist now" (PS, p. 209). Thus the truth, underlying the novels up to and including *Slaughterhouse-Five*, might be seen as the necessity of accepting evil as part of human experience along with the concomitant realizations that "a little touch of suffering makes the whole world kin" and that there is an underlying necessity to love "whoever is around to be loved"; while the truth—similar though different enough to be distinguished from the first and underlying the last six novels through *Bluebeard*—is that human kinship and love may lead again to a vision of the wholeness of life and human beings: a "dream of human communities which are designed to harmonize with what human beings really need and are" (PS, p. 210). It is this resolved vision of human life that underlies the shift in Vonnegut's satire from the bittersweet wisdom of Bokonon in *Cat's Cradle* and the desperate wanderings of Malachi Constant in *The Sirens of Titan* through the dissection of American values in the 1970s and early eighties in *Breakfast of Champions, Jailbird,* and *Deadeye Dick* to the gentle chiding of humanity by Leon Trout in *Galápagos*, until we reach the happy resolution of Robo Karabekian's life in *Bluebeard*. (This "resolved vision" may also very well underlie Vonnegut's own shift from pessimism to optimism.)

This shift in attitude and tone is accompanied by a shift in plot and character that Vonnegut himself predicted. In an interview in 1973, he was asked what he thought would happen in his work in the future. With characteristic understatement, he said:

> My guesses about what I'll write next are based on what has happened to other human beings as they've aged. My intuition will pooh out—my creative craziness; there will be fewer pretty accidents in my writing. I'll become more of an explainer and less of a shower. In order to have enough things to talk about, I may finally have to become more of an

educated man. My career astonishes me. How could anybody have come this far with so little information, with such
garbled ideas of what other writers have said? (WF&G, p.
284).

To write his later novels, he did become in a limited sense
"more of an educated man" in that, besides his earlier research in
World War II for *Mother Night* and *Slaughterhouse-Five,* he later
did research in labor history and the Sacco and Vanzetti trial for
Jailbird, in Darwinian evolution for *Galápagos,* and in art theory
and history for *Bluebeard.*

After first suffering from obscurity and critical neglect for much of
his career,[12] Vonnegut then ironically suffered from popularity. Because he became known first as a writer of science-fiction paperbacks,
then sold so well in uniform editions to such a wide public, many critics refused to take his work seriously.[13] In contrast, by the late eighties, Vonnegut's place among contemporary writers of fiction appears
assured: no longer confined to the debilitating categories of black hu-
morist, science-fiction writer or cult figure, he is instead hailed as an
original voice who devised a telegraphic style best suited to what he
had to say. Translated into several languages, including Russian and
Hungarian, he became a spokesperson for America at home and
abroad in much the same way, but with better insight into the American experience, as television or films are. Finally, he used his fame to
speak out on the important political, social, and environmental issues.

There also has been a certain amount of misreading of
Vonnegut's work because some critics want to find in it something
that simply is not there. For example, Vonnegut distinguishes
himself from those other writers, many of whom he admires, but
whose work is, essentially, part of an on-going series of what he
calls "literary experiments":

> To me, there are some important writers—say, John Barth,
> Donald Barthelme and Jorge Luis Borges—who seem to be
> concentrating on what we could call "literary history," in the
> sense that they're responding to literary experiments in the
> past and are refining them. They're also responding to life,
> of course; I don't mean to imply they aren't. But they have a
> certain academic strain within their works, an awareness of
> being part of an evolutionary scheme, and I don't feel any
> such awareness.[14]

Instead, Vonnegut's books reflect his own involvement with "life." He does this in two ways. 1) He identifies the three questions to which each individual seeks answers: "where he is, what is going on, and what is likely to happen next" (BB, p. 296); and 2) he expresses the major issues of the modern era, including genocide; the destruction of the environment; the various insane methods we have devised for exterminating the human race and all of life in the thin ecosphere; the importance of artistic integrity; the corrosive effects of corruption in government, drugs in society, and racism in the United States; the incredible loneliness Americans experience as the other side of their mobility; the inexplicable nature of money and finance, and the necessity of rejecting the collaboration with evil; and the obligation to love "whoever is around to love" and if that fails, then, to practice courtesy.

In *Breakfast of Champions* Kilgore Trout reads a message scrawled on the wall of a men's room in a New York movie theatre: "What is the purpose of life?" He wishes to respond but, like his son, Leon, in *Galápagos*, finds:

> he had nothing to write with, not even a burnt match. So he left the question unanswered, but here is what he would have written, if he had found anything to write with:

> To be
> the eyes
> and ears
> and conscience
> of the Creator of the Universe,
>   you fool (BC, p. 67).

Vonnegut has spent his life as a professional writer and public person responding to this question and becoming "the eyes and ears and conscience of the Creator of the Universe" through his speaking, his occasional writing, and especially through his fiction. And he has done it all with good humor, a fine comic sense, the absence of any special pleading or of any "academic strain," a considerable narrative skill, and, above all, a truly marvelous "exhuberance of invention."[15]

NOTES

1 *Vonnegut in America*, ed. Jerome Klinkowitz and Donald L. Lawler (New York: Delacorte, 1977), p. 11.

2 See PS, pp. 185-191, 303-310.

3 *The Fictions of Satire* (Baltimore: The Johns Hopkins Press, 1967), p. 21.

4 Cf. Klinkowitz and Lawler, pp. 26-34.

5 *Vonnegut: A Preface to His Novels* (Port Washington: Kennikat Press, 1977), p. 5.

6 Lawrence I. Berkove, "The 'Poor Players' of *Huckleberry Finn*," *Papers of the Michigan Academy of Science, Arts, and Letters* 53 (1968), p.295. Berkove argues convincingly that the whole of Twain's novel hinges on the series of impersonations which in turn leads to a loss of personal freedom, pp. 291-310.

7 "Interview" with John Casey and Joe David Bellamy, in Joe David Bellamy, *The New Fiction: Interviews with Innovative American Writers* (Urbana: University of Illinois Press, 1974), p. 206.

8 "Bonhoeffer Remembered," *Union News* (September 1984), p. 2.

9 Tony Tanner asserts that "Billy Pilgrim . . . takes refuge in an intense fantasy life, which involves his being captured and sent to a remote planet . . . He also comes 'unstuck in time' and present moments during the war may either give way to an intense re-experiencing of moments from the past or unexpected hallucinations of life in the future," but such a stance denies the fantastic premise of Vonnegut's novel: that Billy Pilgrim does indeed move forward and backward in time. One might as well suggest that Gregor Samsa only hallucinates being a cockroach in Kafka's "The Metamorphosis." Neither story makes much sense as an hallucination. Tanner, *City of Words: American Fiction, 1950-1970* (London: Cape, 1971), p. 195.

10 *Modern Satire* (New York: Harcourt Brace Javanovitch, 1962), p. iv.

11 *Science Fiction Today and Tomorrow*, ed. Reginald Bretnor (Baltimore: Penguin, 1974), p. 199.

12 As examples Vonnegut cites the fact that "None of my books were particularly popular when they came out: *Cat's Cradle* and *Mother Night* were never even reviewed." (Charlie Reilly, "Two Conversations with Kurt Vonnegut," *College Literature* 7.1 [Winter 1980], p. 4) "*Esquire* published a list of the American literary world . . . it had made me feel subhuman" (WF&G, pp. 279-280).

13 As late as 1971, critic Max F. Schulz could say with ample justification: "It is no exaggeration to say that his audience has been slow in learning how to read his stories," and goes on to substantiate his case. "The Unconfirmed Thesis: Kurt Vonnegut, Black Humor, and Contemporary Art." *Critique, Studies in Modern Fiction* 12.3 (1971), pp. 7-8.

14 Reilly, 18.

15 Brian Aldiss, *The Trillion Year Spree* (New York: Atheneum, 1986) p. 328.

III. Vonnegut as Messenger: *Slaughterhouse-Five*

"And I alone am escaped to tell you."
The Messenger to Job

Vonnegut wrote *Slaughterhouse-Five* as Joseph Heller wrote *Catch-22*, looking back on the Second World War from a vantage point of twenty to twenty-five years. Unlike Heller, however, what he found to criticize was not "everyone cashing in"—in an ironic moment he even admitted that "one way or another, I got two or three dollars for every person killed [in Dresden]. Some business I'm in" (PS, p. 302)—but rather chose to focus on the brutal, excessive destruction done in the name of goodness, justice, and Mom's apple pie.

In his introduction to the novel, Vonnegut applauds Lot's wife, who in the Old Testament was turned into a pillar of salt for daring to witness the destruction of Sodom and Gomorah, the infamous cities on the plain. "I love her for that," says Vonnegut, "because it was so human" (SH, p. 19). By looking back at the destruction of Dresden, Vonnegut reminds readers that, even in the best of causes against the worst of enemies, human beings have done and apparently will continue to commit the most unimaginable of atrocities. Why? In the Book of Job in the Old Testament, Job long ago found the answer to that question and Vonnegut repeats it for today's readers: "Why?" Why not? Because a person is good does not mean that he or she will escape evil or that he or she is incapable of doing evil. Job's expectation, that evil would not be visited upon a good or an innocent person, was as ill-founded a belief as Vonnegut's or anyone's might be. *Slaughterhouse-Five* suggests, therefore, that evil is beyond human understanding and that the destruction of the innocent and undefended is as common now as when Job bewailed his fate.

For much of his career as a writer and for half his career as a novelist, Kurt Vonnegut wrestled with the terrible moral issue of surviving the destruction of the unarmed city of Dresden in a firestorm in which "The city appeared to boil" (PS, p. 302), leaving 135,000 dead in one night. Such massive destruction is almost beyond human imagining and certainly mind-numbing. About such devastation in *Slaughterhouse-Five*, Vonnegut says:

. . . I felt the need to say this every time a character died: 'So it goes.' This exasperated many critics, and it seemed fancy and tiresome to me, too. But it somehow had to be said.

It was a clumsy way of saying what Celine managed to imply so much more naturally in everything he wrote, in effect: "Death and suffering can't matter nearly as much as I think they do. Since they are so common, my taking them so seriously must mean that I am insane. I must try to be saner" (PS, p. 296).

But how? Having survived the firebombing and what may well be the largest single massacre of European civilian population ever, he returned home after being repatriated as a prisoner of war. Like many of his contemporaries, he had interesting stories to tell of the war and the comraderie he experienced, but again and again he failed to find the right medium for his message about the massacre and whatever it might mean. Unable to passively accept the destruction, he asked the questions all survivors ask, "Why me?" "Why was I allowed to survive?" And parallel to that question, there were all the others: "How could this terrible destruction have been allowed to happen?" "How could human beings do such awful things to one another?" In novel after novel, Vonnegut tries to deal with these questions directly or indirectly. In *The Sirens of Titan*, for example, he probes into history for the answers but finds there nothing but absurdity. In *Mother Night* he examines the possibility of good collaborating with the forces of evil to subvert and ultimately to destroy such forces but has to conclude that this kind of naivete is no match for a truly powerful evil force, such as Fascism. In *Cat's Cradle*, on the other hand, he explores the possibility of stoic cynicism as an answer to the moral dilemma through his splendid creation of Bokonon and Bokononism. Diogenes, the patron saint of cynics, would warmly approve of Bokonon and his view of life as given in the *Books of Bokonon*. If human beings are so hell-bent on their own destruction, then, suggests *Cat's Cradle*, no one or nothing can stop them, and all the novelist can do is warn against the impending disaster.

In *God Bless You, Mr. Rosewater*, Vonnegut tries the opposite tact by examining the effect of doing good works as a way of stopping or at least slowing down the forces of evil. "Sell all you have and give it to the poor" was Jesus' admonition in the first century, so Eliot Rosewater establishes his foundation to give away money. When the phone rings, he answers: "Rosewater Foundation, how may we help you?" and hopes that money may indeed help the person on the other end of the line. But good works ultimately do not appear to really slow evil down. Instead, they actually may encourage it to greater extravagances of connivance and fraud. Evil itself worms its way into the heart of good works and so threatens to destroy the Rosewater Foundation itself until Eliot thwarts it with his preemptive strike by giving away all he has.

In *Slaughterhouse-Five,* Vonnegut at last discovers a way of dealing artistically and personally with "death and suffering" by shifting his perspective from that of human beings to that of God or, in this instance, to that of the Tralfamadoreans. When Billy Pilgrim finds himself in the Tralfamadorean zoo, he asks: "Why me?" The answer he receives both puzzles and instructs him:

"That is a very *Earthling* question to ask, Mr. Pilgrim. Why *you*? . . . Why *anything*? Because this moment simply *is*. . . .

Well, here we are, Mr. Pilgrim trapped in . . . this moment. There is no *why*" (SH, p. 66).

This Tralfamadorean perspective, which Vonnegut adopts, is very similar to God's as pictured in the Book of Job. In the prologue to the Book of Job, messengers come to Job bringing news of horrendous destruction. The first one reveals that all his servants have been killed; the second that his sheep have been destroyed by fire from heaven; the third that nomads have carried off his camels and killed his herdsmen; and the fourth brings the worst news of all: a hurricane suddenly killed all his sons and daughters. Naturally Job is heartstricken. He rends his clothes and goes and sits on the village dunghill in deep mourning. While there, he receives visits from three friends who attempt to comfort him with conventional wisdom arguing that evil occurs because a person has done evil. Job claims, rightly, that he is innocent, God-fearing, and has done only good. The second friend contends that evil occurs because a person neglects to perform certain required ceremonies or religious duties, and if only Job will repent and perform them, all will be well. But again Job says that he is a model of piety and has left no ceremony unobserved nor any duty unperformed. The third friend then argues that evil never occurs without a reason, and, therefore, if destruction has been visited upon Job, then, that is ipso facto proof that Job is indeed guilty of something. If he will but "search his heart" to discover his mistake and repent of it, then, all will be well. But Job has done nothing wrong. As Jesus was to say a few centuries later, "The rain falls on the just and the unjust," and because a hurricane destroys people or property is no reason to believe such people were guilty of any wrong-doing. Nature is notoriously neutral and is, therefore, an unreliable guide to human goodness or evil. Writing "A Letter to the Next Generation" in an "Open Forum" series of advertisements sponsored by Volkswagen, Vonnegut concludes by giving a lengthy list of natural disasters and saying: "If people think Nature is their friend, then they sure don't need an enemy." In other words, do not look to Nature for moral guidance.

Job's tragedy is that he is a good man who experienced great evil—exactly as Dresden was a "good" city, an "open," unarmed civilian city whose architectural beauty was legendary. Yet Dresden was destroyed though undefended "to hasten the end of the war" (SH, p. 155), as Job's innocent sons and daughters were destroyed to "teach Job a lesson." By the end of the book, Job accepts the imperfection of the world and his inability to account for the evil in it. As the man of faith, he also comes to accept the goodness of his Creator, although that goodness may not always be apparent in the less than perfect world in which he must live. He states simply, "I believe; help Thou mine unbelief," which is the heartfelt cry of all believers in a Diety.

Vonnegut, as a rational atheist, can find none of the consolation that Job found in the answers of traditional faith. He can and does find some consolation, however, in accepting an imperfect world where the power of evil to destroy is real and often terrifying, but where the power of reason and goodness is also real and occasionally even wins out over evil. As a character in a Bertolt Brecht play says, "In the worst of times, there are good people." So Eliot Rosewater gives all he has away, and Malachi Constant at long last learns "to love whoever is around to be loved." In *Slaughterhouse-Five*, Billy Pilgrim becomes the chief attraction in a zoo on another planet in another galaxy where he and Montana Wildhack are put on exhibit as interesting specimens of an endangered species. Although their captors have long ago concluded, based upon thousands of years of observation, that the most prominent characteristic of human beings appears to be their ability to self-destruct, these two copulate and produce an off-spring while in the zoo, thus illustrating humanity's drive to continue the race which may help to counterbalance its drive to destroy it. (Compare *Deadeye Dick*, p. 185.) This modest hopefulness is a far cry from the total despair experienced by Mona, the incredibly beautiful woman of the Sunday supplements who, as the world ends in *Cat's Cradle*, refuses to make love to Jonah-John because "that's how babies are made" and no sane person would want to have a child as the world ends. But Montana Wildhack and Billy Pilgrim, less worldly-wise and far more childlike, under much less favorable conditions in the Tralfamadorean zoo, amidst their Sears Roebuck furnishings, copulate and reproduce to the delight and glee of their audience. Perhaps that suggests Earth's ultimate function in the universe: to puzzle and delight extraterrestial on-lookers who visit this planet with the paradox of humans who both reproduce—that is, give life—and destroy themselves—that is, take life—at one and the same time. So it goes.

In his role as the "messenger to Job," besides dealing with the "commonness" of death, Vonnegut also attempts to account for unmotivated human suffering, such as that caused by the incineration of 135,000 people in Dresden, by pointing to the accidental nature of life. Some of this reasoning will be familiar from *The Sirens of Titan* in which the Space Traveller maintains that "I was the victim of a series of accidents. ... As are we all," but here there is an important difference: in *The Sirens of Titan* the accidents are actually caused by visitors from Tralfamadore who manipulated all human history for their own ends. Worse, as Salo, the messenger, points out, these visitors are not even human beings or sentient creatures, but are machines. In contrast, in *Slaughterhouse-Five* there is no one using or abusing human history for any purpose whatsoever nor is anything or anyone in control. Rather than wrestle further with the issue of "purpose" or lack of it, Vonnegut replaces the question, "Why me?" with its twin question to which there is no reply: "Why not you?" Questions also posed in the conclusion of the Book of Job first by Elihu, then by God, as each asks Job in turn: "Why did you expect that your goodness would give you immunity from the effects of evil or from accidents of nature?" There is no such immunity for human beings. Good people suffer and bad people suffer since "The rain falls on the just and the unjust." Suffering, by itself, is no measure either of a person's evil—as Job's three friends had mistakenly maintained—nor of a person's goodness—as Job had assumed. Suffering simply is a part of this world and all human experience, and no divine force will interfere in human history to stop it: ". . . the little Lord Jesus/ No crying He makes" (SH epigraph, n.p.).

The thought behind Vonnegut's novel could, therefore, be called a challenging, if fairly orthodox, form of Judeo-Christian theology. No wonder school boards and other official bodies whose members rarely read, much less comprehend, the books which they ban or burn, have attacked it and once, at least, in Drake, North Dakota, *"Slaughter-house-Five* was actually burned in a furnace by a school janitor . . . on instructions from the school commitee"![1] It threatened their comfortable view of the world and religion exactly as the Book of Job, the Old Testament Prophets, and Jesus's Sermon on the Mount did hundreds of years ago. In all these books, as in *Slaughterhouse-Five*, the terms "punishment" and "reward" it turns out, do not make a lot of sense from the human, but only from the divine perspective. In such a world, why would anyone do good rather than evil? A good person, according to the Book of Job and Judeo-Christian belief, is simply a good person and the only reason for being good rather than evil is because that is who and what a good person is; thus, a good person is someone who does good which is its own reward. Someone who is evil, on the other hand, is simply someone who does evil, which is its own punishment.

None of Vonnegut's characters, including those in *Slaughter-house-Five*, are evil, but they are rather human beings to whom accidents happen. Most are innocent. Vonnegut's father once said to him, ". . . you never wrote a story with a villain in it" (SH, p. 7). Billy Pilgrim is neither John Wayne, riding into the sunset to save Western civilization from the Fascists, nor Jesus preaching the necessity of "doing good to those who do evil to you." Instead he is a soldier in war and a child in peace, who neatly illustrates Celine's observation that "When not actually killing, your soldier's a child." The identity of soldiers as children is also reflected in the subtitle of *Slaughterhouse-*

Five: or The Children's Crusade, which links the great war to end all wars with one of the most futile, exploitive, cynical events in all of western European history: the Children's Crusade—a crusade that never went anywhere and never accomplished anything, except to provide ample prey upon which all kinds of human vultures fed.

In *Slaughterhouse-Five* the soldiers in World War II, like the children on the crusade, had little or no idea about what they were doing and often did not know even where they were. It was the generals who planned such glorious operations as the destruction of Dresden (see SH, pp.161-62). The reduction of a monument of human civilization, such as the city on the Elbe, to a pile of rubble overnight or the metamorphosis of hundreds-of-thousands of un-armed people into a "corpse factory" can, and, indeed, has hap-pened in "a world where "everything is permitted." In such a world, says Ivan Karamazov in *The Brothers Karamazov,* the issue is not whether to believe in God or not; it is the horror of the power of evil. Yet, as Eliot Rosewater, who also "found life meaningless, partly because of what [he] . . . had seen in war," says to Billy Pil-grim: "everything there was to know about life was in *The Brothers Karamazov* ... 'But that isn't *enough* any more' ..." (SH, p. 87). And so perhaps all we can do is to follow Theodore Roethke's advice, which Vonnegut quotes with approval, to "learn by going where [we] . . . have to go" (SH, p. 18). Dresden, one of the most beautiful of all the German, of all the European cities was obliterated in one night with virtually all the people living there:

> When the Americans and their guards did come out [next noontime after the firestorm], the sky was black with smoke. The sun was an angry little pinhead. Dresden was like the moon now, nothing but minerals. The stones were hot. Ev-erybody else in the neighborhood was dead (SH, p. 153).
> What do you say after a massacre? "Everything is sup-posed to be very quiet after a massacre, and it always is, ex-cept for the birds. And what do the birds say? All there is to say about a massacre, things like "Poo-tee-weet?" (SH, p. 17).

If the slaughterhouse itself, from which the novel takes its title, was once a house of death, it became, paradoxically during the inferno of the Dresden firebombing, a house of salvation when it gave oxygen to its occupants rather than to the firestorm. Similarly, while Vonnegut's novel is an account of the worst massacre of unarmed civilians in modern Europe, it is also a plea for a change in values and attitudes which would make other such massacres impossible. One way it accomplishes this task is by making the massacre itself public knowledge, for the novel brought it back into living memory in a way that could not be ignored, a portion of American history which had never officially been acknowledged, and which had been either inadvertently or deliberately concealed. According to Vonnegut in the "twenty-seven-volume *Official History of the Army Air Force in World War Two* ... there was almost nothing ... about the Dresden raid, even though it had been such a howling success. The extent of the success had been kept a secret for many years after the war—a secret from the American people" (SH, p. 165).

William Butler Yeats, the Nobel Prize winning poet, once said that "a poet writes out of his personal life [and] in his finest work out of its tragedy, whatever it be . . .." Vonnegut implies that *Slaughterhouse-Five* is the result of his "dance with death" without which he says, quoting Celine with approval, "no art is possible" (SH, p. 18). Thus he writes out of the "tragedy" he experienced, which raised acutely the profound moral issues with which he has had to wrestle as an adult human being and as a writer. Perhaps that also helps account for the relief he felt in finishing it: "I felt," he says, "after I finished *Slaughterhouse-Five* that I didn't have to write at all anymore if I didn't want to. It was the end of some sort of career" (WF&G, p. 280).

Clearly Vonnegut has written movingly, compellingly out of the tragedy he experienced in Dresden and for many—perhaps, for most—of his readers, *Slaughterhouse-Five* remains his finest work: an impressive achievement whether looked at as a human document or as a work of art. Robert Scholes sums up the qualities of the novel that contribute to its success:

> It is funny, compassionate, and wise. The humor in
> Vonnegut's fiction is what enables us to contemplate the
> horror that he finds in contemporary existence. It does not
> disguise the awful things perceived; it merely strengthens

29

and comforts us to the point where such perception is bearable. Comedy can look into depths which tragedy dares not acknowledge.[2]

After wrestling with some of the most profound and some of the most difficult human questions in *Slaughterhouse-Five*, Vonnegut promised himself: "The next one I write is going to be fun" (SH, p. 19), which certainly proved true in the wild comedy of *Breakfast of Champions*. It would be almost twenty years before he would return to these issues raised for him by World War II and, in *Bluebeard*, present a picture of the end of the war in Europe as a field crowded with people: the lunatics, the refugees, the war prisoners, the concentration camp victims—all the ragged remnants of an exhausted world, but more important: all survivors—and living human beings, rather than the stacked corpses of the Hospital of Hope and Mercy in *Cat's Cradle* or the "corpse mine" found in the desolate Dresden landscape of *Slaughterhouse-Five*. But that novel is another twenty years in the future after this one. For now it is enough that Vonnegut— the messenger—could bring news of the disaster together with the resulting examination of issues central to all human experience: the question of the power of evil, the awareness of inhuman destruction, and the omnipresence of human suffering.

NOTES

1 PS, p. 4. See also PS, pp. 3-17. In a "Dear Friend" letter written to solicit funds for the ACLU (The American Civil Liberties Union), Vonnegut reveals that *Slaughterhouse-Five* is among the ten "most frequently censored [and banned] books" in public schools and libraries. Others in the top ten include John Steinbeck, *The Grapes of Wrath* and *Of Mice and Men*, Judy Blume, *Forever*, and Mark Twain, *Huckleberry Finn*. "Kurt Vonnegut," undated letter, pp. 2-3.
2 *Fabulation and Metafiction* (Urbana: University of Illinois Press, 1979), p. 204.

IV. No Survivors: The Early Novels
Player Piano, The Sirens of Titan, Mother Night, Cat's Cradle, God Bless You, Mr. Rosewater

"The Implications Were Sensational"
Player Piano

The success of *Slaughterhouse-Five* led to the reprinting of Vonnegut's early novels and more importantly to their being reread, discussed, and some of them being reviewed seriously for the first time. These five novels, *Player Piano, The Sirens of Titan, Mother Night, Cat's Cradle,* and *God Bless You, Mr. Rosewater*—the last four of which were written within only about six years—represent a significant accomplishment: each is distinctive, yet each is recognizably Vonnegut's; each breaks new thematic and conceptual ground; and each attempts to deal with a major moral, social, or political issue.

Vonnegut's first novel, *Player Piano,* is one of several that appeared in the last forty years sounding the alarm over the dangers of automation. Set in the near future, the familiar plot was "borrowed" from Aldous Huxley's *Brave New World,* but Huxley in his turn, says Vonnegut, "borrowed" it from Samiatan's *We* (WF&G, p. 261).

Besides extrapolating from the present to create a future society, Vonnegut adds a satiric, highly amused look at the morés of the corporate world that he knew intimately from his work at General Electric. Having an excellent ear for dialect, conversation, and various forms of human speech, Vonnegut easily parodies the pompous letter-writing style of bureaucrats, the inflated rhetoric of overly intellectual leaders, the cheerleader style of corporate executives, the street dialect of various down-and-outs. He also satirizes the kind of husband-wife relationship that the corporation expects and even requires of its employees. The toll such rituals take, can be seen in the cliché-ridden, meaningless conversations which take place daily between Paul Proteus, upwardly mobile, aspiring young husband, and his wife, Anita—"Illium's Lady of the Manor"—who spends all her time and energy plotting and attempting to boost him up the corporate ladder. Vonnegut's sharp satiric eye neatly scewers his target as Anita dresses Paul for success by buying clothing identical with that of those a bit further up the corporate ladder and coaches him on all his moves, meetings and speeches. One of the targets Vonnegut hit directly was the North Woods summer festival where GE executives had to go and play the silly games described in *Player Piano*. "The island was shut down after the book [PP] came out," recalls Vonnegut.[1] "So, you can't say that my writing hasn't made any contribution to Western civilization.[2]

Juxtaposed to the corporate world is Homestead where ex-workers and those with minimal jobs live and where revolt may be incipient but life is as dead as it is at the top. Here there is no dignity in labor, no virtue in an honest day's wages, no reward for exceeding expectations. Instead these people realize that the corporate world wishes to use their labor as cheaply as possible, to replace them with more reliable machines whenever and wherever possible, and will not stop to count the human cost. Much of this theme of the exploited human or of machines taking over work leaving behind a pile of human rubble with little or nothing to do is familiar from some 19th—and many 20th—century British writers, for example, Ruskin, Hardy, Lawrence, Forster and Tolkien, and from Mark Twain and the muckrakers in the United States. Vonnegut's handling of the subject has the ring of truth, in part, because he lived and worked in the atmosphere he describes and, in part, because as he says, "it was a genuine concern that drove me to write my first book."[3] He recounts that at GE:

> One day I came across an engineer who had developed a milling machine that could be run by punch cards. Now at the time, milling machine operators were among the best paid machinists in the world, and yet this damned machine was able to do as good a job as most of the machinists ever could. I looked around, then, and found looms and spinning machines and a number of textile devices all being run the same way and, well, the implications were sensational.[4]

In *Player Piano* a future, electronic society places the good of the corporation and the full employment of machines ahead of human needs and desires. In *The Sirens of Titan* Vonnegut explores this issue further through the ultimate machine-run civilization of Tralfamador, a planet whose people made machines to do the work of human beings:

> This left the creatures free to serve higher purposes. But whenever they found a higher purpose, the purpose still wasn't high enough.
>
> So machines were made to serve higher purposes, too.
>
> And the machines did everything so expertly that they were finally given the job of finding out what the higher purpose of the creatures [humans] could be.
>
> The machines reported in all honesty that the creatures couldn't really be said to have any purpose at all.
>
> The creatures thereupon began slaying each other. . . .
>
> [And they discovered that they weren't even very good at slaying. So they turned that job over to the machines, too. And the machines finished up the job in less time than it takes to say, "Tralfamadore" (ST, pp. 274-75).

As the Hungarian critic Zoltán Abadi-Nágy notes: "Constant's view of transcendental control [is] . . . deflated when Tralfamadore turns out to be a dehumanized planet with a machine civilization: what *they* can teach man is that man should not learn from them."[5]

In *Player Piano* the world, having passed through the First Revolution when machines took over man's manual labor, and the Second Revolution when machines took over all routine work, is now about to undergo a Third Revolution when machines will do all their thinking for them. The huge computer, EPICAC XIV sitting in the Carlsbad Caverns in Colorado, determines all of the country's needs from the number of refrigerators this month to the kinds of books people should read to the types of educational degrees universities may offer. This governing by computer results in an increasingly sterile American society, which has no real place for humans and where a visitor from another culture correctly identifies all the citizens as "*Takaru*" or slaves. The hero, Paul Proteus, tries but does not really succeed in becoming his own person, a free man. When he isn't being used by the corporation or his wife, then he is being used by the revolutionaries who write letters in his name, issue manifestoes with which he is not sure he agrees, and act generally as if he was their Messiah—something he definitely does not wish to be. If he doesn't really know what he wants to be or do, he at least knows that he does not want to be a manager who oversees machines.

Vonnegut's book is a plea for human beings to be what they are able to be best: human—that is, frail and strong, stupid and intelligent, cruel and kind, failing and succeeding, hating and loving. (This belief in the humanness of human beings will become a constant in all of Vonnegut's later novels and stories.) In *Player Piano* the corporation opposes this belief in the variety of humans and their experiences, for it desires to make everything as easy as possible for everyone. But, as the Irish writer Francis Stuart observes, "Where everything is seen as making life easier for all, there is no room for grief, pain and doubt, in which are the roots of a thriving organic consciousness."[6] Paul Proteus's flailing about, trying to be at home in Homestead, buying a farm that he cannot run, and attempting to be the Messiah of the saboteurs, reflects his blind desire to become a conscious being, to become fully human. The corporation, on the other hand, wants him to be its ideal manager—bright, but completely within the corporate mold. His wife wants him to be her ideal husband—loving but totally dedicated to succeeding in the corporation. The revolutionary Ghost Shirts want him to be their ideal leader—famous, but selflessly dedicated to their cause. None wants him simply to be or to be for himself alone, and no one ever asks what he wants. The wonder is that he does not become like his fellow workers: alcoholics, drop-outs, or flunkies—the hollow shells of the wasted.

If Vonnegut had written no novels after *Player Piano*, and it would be almost eight years before he attempted another, it probably would have today an appreciative, though small audience. Because of his phenomenal success with *Slaughterhouse-Five* and several other novels, many readers enjoy reading it with hindsight from those other novels. For instance, the awareness of the "uselessness" of human beings, which lies at the core of this novel, is also central to several short stories and later becomes the pivotal question in *God Bless You, Mr. Rosewater*. And the question, which the Shah in *Player Piano* wishes to pose to the giant computer, "What people are for?" (PP, p. 302) will reoccur in the Kilgore Trout novel, 2BRO2B, spoken by a customer to the hostess of the Ethical Suicide Parlor where he has gone to die, "What in hell are people for?" (GB, pp. 21-22).

In itself, *Player Piano* remains a skillfully written novel that holds readers' interest, reflects decent, humane values, incorporates some wonderfully comic sections, and, overall, reflects the satiric thrust which will mark all of Vonnegut's later writing.

History and the Dehumanization Process
The Sirens of Titan

The Sirens of Titan, a brilliantly inventive work, reveals not only Vonnegut's potential as a comic writer of future fiction, but also his accomplishment in conceiving and executing a dazzling, fast-paced tour of the solar system containing memorable incidents, characters, and language that focus on the significant problem of the meaning or lack of it in human history. As one critic remarks: "*Sirens* is easily Vonnegut's most flamboyant novel, with its entire universe at the mercy of the 'outrageous fortune' that operates in varying degrees in all of Vonnegut's [early] novels."[7]

The danger of *The Sirens of Titan* is, however, that readers will be so overwhelmed by its "flamboyancy," by the frenetic activity of the plot, that they may overlook its other qualities. For the great tour of the planets of the solar system, the war between the two worlds, the violent social changes necessitated by the nightmare of equality and irrelevance—all are only the means Vonnegut uses to explore human inner space, and the question of essential human worth. (A question which dominates much of his early writing through *Slaughterhouse-Five*.) Within all the activity, Vonnegut introduces the motif of the Quest, one of the oldest of all metaphors for human experience. Almost always in his novels, there is a false quest for the meaning *of* life juxtaposed to the true quest for the meaning *in* life. In *Cat's Cradle*, for example, Bokonon warns the faithful against this pitfall through several sacred calypsos, especially this one:

Tiger got to hunt,
Bird got to fly;
Man got to sit and wonder, "why, why why?"
Tiger got to sleep,
Bird got to land;
Man got to tell himself he understand (CC, p. 124).

Vonnegut once told how, at the beginning of each writing class he teaches, he lays down one firm rule: "All you can do is tell what happened," he admonishes his students. "You will get thrown out of this course if you are arrogant enough to imagine that you can tell me why it happened. You do not know. You cannot know" (PS, p. 189). Characters in his novels who violate this rule and attempt to discover why something happened, such as Malachi Constant in *The Sirens of Titan*, pay for it dearly. Yet his characters are continually, to use his word, "embarrassed" that they do not understand. In *The Sirens of Titan*, for example, God is known by his absence and indifference to human problems. Therefore, he is best worshipped through the rituals of the Church of God the Utterly Indifferent—a highly popular sect in this "true story from the Nightmare Ages, falling roughly, give or take a few years, between the Second World War and the Third Great Depression" (ST, p. 8). Early in the novel, Constant, the richest man in the world, asserts in opposition to God's indifference: ". . . somebody up there likes me" (ST, p. 20). (A phrase Vonnegut may have borrowed from the title of a world heavyweight champion's biography.) Time teaches Constant a different lesson so that when he appears at last as the Space Wanderer wearing an improbable bright yellow suit decorated with huge "orange question marks a foot high," he proclaims: "I WAS A VICTIM OF A SERIES OF ACCIDENTS, AS ARE WE ALL" (ST, p. 229). In other words: "You do not know. You cannot know . . . why it happened."

Perhaps what Kafka meant in his aphorism, "The world was made on one of God's bad days," is that the Diety neglected to include a moral order that human beings could appreciate or, at least, perceive. Characters in Vonnegut's fiction who search for such an order in the universe or for the meaning of life, whether moral, political or omnipotent, are doomed to fail. A more human and, therefore, more appropriate stance would be to stop pretending to understand what cannot be understood and simply confess bemusement. When his own children would ask him, "Why?" his standard rebuttal was: "I just got here myself" (PS, p. 177).

There is an ancient story in Zen Buddhism that illustrates Vonnegut's point: a master-teacher instructed his pupil: "if you meet the Buddha on the road kill him!" Such advice, even from such an excellent source shocked and mystified the pupil until, after giving it long thought, he understood: it is necessary that each individual discover the truth that life holds for him or her alone and not take another's truth for his or her own, not even from the Buddha himself. Similarly, in John Bunyan's *The Pilgrim's Progress,* which for a long time was the most read book in English after the Bible, the point is made that the nature and goal of any quest becomes apparent not in the beginning, but only during the journey, and then mostly at the end. The hero, Christian, before he sets out, has very little notion of where he is going. Nor are there any reliable maps of the territory. His guide, Evangelist, in attempting to give him directions to the Heavenly City of Salvation, asks him:

Do you see yonder wicket-gate? The man [Christian] said, No. Then said the other, Do you see yonder shining light? He said, I think I do. Then said Evangelist, Keep that light in your eye, and go up directly thereto: so shalt thou see the gate . . ."[8]

In *Slaughterhouse-Five* Vonnegut quotes with approval Theodore Roethke in much the same vein: "I learn by going where I have to go." When Malachi Constant in *The Sirens of Titan* believes that he knows exactly where he is going and what he is doing, then, he is in the greatest danger of missing the meaning in life. As Vonnegut once quipped: "thinking that the guy up ahead knows what he is doing is the most dangerous delusion there is."

Constant wanted to find "a single message that was sufficiently dignified and important to merit his carrying it humbly between two points" (ST, p. 17). His prayer appears answered when he gets to carry a message, but in the end it proves to be not what he really wanted or needed, so he lands in despair. For while his message, which lies at the heart of *The Sirens of Titan,* is a truly important one, it is hardly "dignified" nor is it really his; that is, it does not mean anything to him. Rather than becoming a true messenger, he is merely used as an errand boy.

Moreover, Constant's errand is a fool's errand: to travel throughout the solar system to deliver the spare part for a Tralfamadorean messenger's broken-down spaceship. The messenger, Salo, has been waiting for this part throughout all of human history. For him, it represents " . . .the culmination of Earthling history . . . the mysterious something that every Earthling was trying so desperately, so earnestly, so gropingly, so exhaustingly to produce and deliver" (ST, p.

37

297). What Constant delivers is his son's "good luck" piece that almost all Earthlings living in the United States would recognize immediately as a "church key"—a beercan and bottle opener. All human history struggled to give birth to this "mouse," this trivial gadget which, whatever else it may be and no matter how important it may be for the Tralfamadorean, hardly qualifies as the "meaning of life," the "dignified" message Constant sought all his life to deliver nor does Constant gain anything by delivering it. As one of Vonnegut's most perceptive critics, Richard Giannone concludes: "The further we go into space [in ST], the more trivial the universe becomes, until finally, beyond the rim from Talfamadore, it all becomes a joke, a shaggy-dog story that tediously adds pointless afterthoughts."[9]

Only after Constant gives up this false quest to deliver a "dignified and important" message—that is, after he gives up searching for the meaning *of* life, and after he "kills" the Buddha who told him to be a messenger—does he discover the meaning *in* life or what life holds for him; which is "to love whoever is around to be loved" (ST, p. 313). Such is the simple end of his complex inner quest for peace and the feeling of self-worth.

On Titan, one of Saturn's moons, Constant has a purpose in life and feels truly "at home," which he never did flitting about the solar system. Still nothing he discovers remotely answers the question, "why?" The narrator ignoring Constant's original motivation, justifiably concludes: "It was all so sad. But it was all so beautiful, too" (ST, p. 305). But it is sadness and beauty at a price, for few readers will overlook other incidents and characters in the book which are cruel, horrifying and ugly, such as the separation of Winston Niles Rumfoord and his dog, Kysack.[10] After being mercilessly used to bring to a conclusion the Grand Scheme of the Tralfamadoreans, dog and man are blown apart by an explosion in the sun. "A Universe schemed in mercy would have kept dog and man together," but comments the narrator, "the Universe inhabited by ... Rumfoord and his dog was not schemed in mercy. Kazak had been sent ahead of his master on the great mission to nowhere and nothing" (ST, p. 295). Thus Vonnegut suggests, as Gary Wolfe succinctly puts it, that "the harsh realities of meaningless cruelty and death . . . will follow man wherever he goes, whatever he does ... because they are a part of what makes him human."[11]

This uncompromising view of the random violence of the universe and the limitations of all human beings combined with the sadness and beauty along with its flamboyant comedy, and ironic use of the quest motif gives *The Sirens of Titan* its special quality.

"That Simple and Widespread Boon
—Schizophrenia"
Mother Night

Mother Night, "the confessions of Howard W. Campbell, Jr." the only reliable American agent still operating in Nazi Germany and still alive at the end of the war, is a study in the schizophrenic personality.[12] To be successful as a spy Campbell had to become a thoroughly convincing Nazi which he accomplished in part by becoming a larger than life Nazi who out-Nazied the Nazis. But because of the inherently crazy Nazi mental structure, all his actions, speeches, broadcasts, and proposals, which in another setting would appear instantly absurd, were taken seriously, often adopted and usually praised. No matter what suggestion Campbell makes to the Third Reich, the response is always the same: wonderful! Let's do it! In 1941, for example, he drew what he thought was an absurdly grotesque "caricature of a cigar-smoking Jew" to be used in target practice (MN, p. 117). Out of "an excess of zeal," he says, "I drew the monster in order to establish myself even more solidly as a Nazi. I overdrew it, with an effect that would have been ludicrous anywhere but in Germany . . ., and I drew it far more amateurishly than I really draw." He continues: "It succeeded nonetheless. I was flabbergasted by its success" (MN, p. 118).

Millions of copies of his target were distributed for which he was well paid including "a bonus of a ten-pound ham, thirty gallons of gasoline, and a week's all-expense-paid vacation for my wife and myself . . ." (MN, p. 118). Another time in New York some sixteen or eighteen years after the war, listening to one of his World War II propaganda broadcasts, he simply could not believe that anyone would take them seriously they are so exaggerated. Yet his immediate highly paranoid audience takes them just as seriously as the German hierarchy or his father-in-law had earlier. It is as if the projector of

Swift's "A Modest Proposal"—who ironically suggested that Ireland solve its problem of a starving, poor population by raising children to be butchered for meat at two years old—not only had his proposal accepted, but his notorious scheme succeeded so well that he was then asked to propose another!

The highest, if most bitterly ironic compliment Campbell received for his work came from his father-in-law who told him on the eve of the fall of Berlin that he once suspected him of being a spy, but that did not matter since: " . . . you could never have served the enemy [America] as well as you served us. . . . almost all the ideas that I hold now, that makes me unashamed of anything I may have felt or done as a Nazi, came not from Hitler, not from Goebbels, not from Himmler— but from you. . . . You alone kept me from concluding that Germany had gone insane" (MN, p. 75). In other words, Campbell, in attempting to establish his trustworthiness, actually furthered the Nazi cause by providing what it most needed and lacked: an intellectual and logical underpinning that gives it the appearance of intellectual and moral respectability. Frank Wertanen, who recruited Campbell as an American spy, maintains that Campbell was indeed a Nazi, for there was no other way he could be so successful in convincing his superiors of his zeal. When Campbell vigorously protests, "That wasn't me." Wirtanen, startled by his sharpness, replies: "Whoever it was—. . . he was one of the most vicious sons of bitches who ever lived." When Campbell again protests, "How else could I have survived?" Wirtanen's answer leaves no room for argument: "That was your problem.. . . Very few men could have solved it as thoroughly as you did." When Campbell asks, "You think I was a Nazi?" Wirtanen, without hesitation, answers: "Certainly you were. How else could a responsible historian classify you?" (MN, p. 143)

Finally, Campbell has nothing and no one for whom to live. Realizing the truth, he is disgusted by what he has become: "That part of me that wanted to tell the truth got turned into an expert liar! The lover in me got turned into a pornographer! The artist in me got turned into ugliness such as the world has rarely seen before. Even my most cherished memories have been converted into catfood, glue and liverwurst!" (MN, p. 156). Campbell took the advice given to Conrad's Lord Jim "in the destructive element immerse," and found that neither he nor his most cherished thoughts, feelings, possessions, or relationships remained untouched. So he sits in his cell in an Israeli jail writing his memoirs and arguing with himself about history and his place in it, much as Eichmann had earlier. His recitation leads inevitably to the schizoid conclusion identical to the historian's: he was in word and deed a Nazi exactly as he was in word and deed the most reliable and only surviving American agent in the Berlin power structure.

In 1966 Vonnegut wrote a new introduction for *Mother Night* in which he says: "This is the only story of mine whose moral I know .. .: We are what we pretend to be, so we must be careful about what we pretend to be" (MN, p. v). Campbell "pretended" to be in the service of the Fascists, but in his "pretending" he became "what he pretended to be." Can one evaluate a lifetime by one single action? asks a character in Sartre's *No Exit*. The answer is, "yes." Campbell learned to his sorrow that he could indeed serve two masters, but at the huge price of becoming split into two people: a superb German Nazi and a superb American spy. By dividing himself so violently, he left no solid identity for himself. By becoming the servant of the Nazis and the servant of the Americans, he left no room for himself as a human being.

Campbell is a double personality, a person split in two. Probably the most famous explorations of the double personality in English literature are Mary Shelley's *Frankenstein*, Robert Louis Stevenson's *Dr. Jekyll and Mr. Hyde,* and Oscar Wilde's *The Picture of Dorian Gray*.[13] Each suggests the dangers in exploring the dark side of the personality, of acknowledging that the human being is not one, but two, and in each case the hero in these three novels destroys himself. In the twentieth century, Carl Jung also studied the dark side, the "shadow" which, he believed, each person must acknowledge and accept to become fully human. Campbell will not and does not embrace this dark side since he erroneously believes that he can simply "pretend" to be it, to play at being his dark double. When what he "pretends" becomes reality, he commits suicide having nothing left to live for, having no good self to become.

Another one of the novel's morals, according to Vonnegut's introduction, is "Make love when you can. It's good for you" (MN, p. vii). Campbell spent a good part of the war making love to his beloved wife,

Helga. Together they formed a "Nation of Two," which became the title of a play he wrote. But his dream of a "nation of two" is false because, unlike the *duprass* of Ambassador Horlick Minton and his wife in *Cat's Cradle* (which is an ideal relationship), Campbell and his wife relate to no one and nothing outside themselves. Failing to become responsible human beings and failing to acknowledge any ties to the human community, their island of love becomes a no man's land for none. She ends up dead somewhere; he takes his life "for crimes against himself." His "editor" concludes that he was "a man who served evil too openly and good too secretly, the crime of his times" (MN, p. xii).

One of Vonnegut's points is, however, that Campbell's case is not unique: most of the characters in the book have wildly conflicting double identities. Kraft is, he says, a retired paint and wallpaper dealer from Indianapolis, but he also proves to be an unsuccessful Russian spy who will go to jail eventually and, while there, become an important modern painter. Resi Noth impersonates her dead older sister Helga, only to find that she has taken her place so completely that her new self leaves no room for her old identity. The Russian Bodov, who plagiarizes Campbell's literary works to get rich quickly, succumbs and becomes a writer himself who makes the costly error of writing satire against the Russian state—a crime for which he pays with his life.

Labelling the insanity that gripped the world for the better part of a decade "schizophrenia" helps Vonnegut locate and dissect the disease to warn his readers against it. ". . . Howard W. Campbell was an authentically bad man," as Vonnegut elsewhere says, and as such is a clear warning against the power of even the most ludicrous distortions about people and values.[14] For evil does not appear pure and clear. As Campbell says to O'Hare, "Where's evil? It's that large part of every man that wants to hate without limit, that wants to hate with God on its side" (MN, p. 190)—whether such hatred is directed against a people, country, cause, or religion. Although Campbell comes too late to self-realization, he does at long last painfully arrive there, whereas his self-righteous captor, Bernard V. O'Hare, does not. Yet O'Hare was on the right side, the American side in the war; appeared on the right magazine cover, LIFE magazine; and does a good patriotic deed when he captures the notorious Campbell—not once, but twice. Still he proves to be part of the hate, ugliness, and horror that bred the war itself. Vonnegut warns that hatred without limits and the resulting mindless violence occur whenever the self-righteous are let loose—whether in Nazi Germany or contemporary America—and worse, will become sanctioned national policy when the self-righteous seize control of a country—any country.

For real self-righteousness involves a divorce from reality and the human, fallible self. Campbell becomes, therefore, a perfect narrator for Vonnegut's theme: the real enemy of humanity is a human being divorced from himself, a schizophrenic, an insane person. Whether that person participates in the ludicrous Nazi beliefs or in mindless hatred of things German and Japanese fostered in America during the war. When World War II ended, many people were puzzled by the United States' new international "friends" who were no longer monsters, but were human beings with families and plans and hopes just like those of Americans. In *Mother Night* a nameless policeman tells about his brother's recent visit to Japan. He reports that "the Japanese were the nicest people he ever met, and [adds the puzzled policeman] it was the Japanese who'd killed our father! Think about that for a minute" (MN, p. 179).

Vonnegut once remarked in a conversation recorded at the University of Iowa that this novel was the most difficult for him to write of his first three because the material "was more personally disturbing to me."[15] He did not mean that he had been tempted to become a spy because "espionage offers each spy an opportunity to go crazy in a way he finds irresistible" (MN, p. 145), but rather that he had to reconsider all aspects of the War having survived the destruction of Dresden, the largest massacre of civilians in modern history, caused not by the evil side, "Them," but by the good side, "Us." As Pogo said: "We have met the enemy and he is us"—a real human being with a human face and with human hopes and needs similar to our own, and not a caricature of a human being whether Communist or Nazi, Gentile or Jew, Japanese, German or American. Such thoughts do not "breed serenity"—Vonnegut's wry comment on novel writing ("Two Conversations," p. 23).

Mother Night is a brilliant study in ". . . that simple and widespread boon to modern mankind—schizophrenia" (MN, p. 136). Using war and espionage as basic metaphors, Vonnegut explores the nature

43

of personality, values and reality—all of which appear contingent upon having and maintaining a clear human identity. This novel about the power of lies may help unmask some of the worst ones as well as help people face some uncomfortable truths about themselves, the countries they live in and those values they call "true" or "good."

Apocalypse Now
Cat's Cradle

The plot of *Cat's Cradle* is a bitterly ironic joke—perhaps, the ultimate joke—of human beings hell-bent on extinguishing all life on Earth because of their greed and stupidity. Although *Player Piano* had many fine comic moments—such as the invention of the Shah's language that sounds vaguely obscene when spoken aloud; the recasting of the patriotic slogan, "Eternal Vigilence Is the Price of Liberty" into "Eternal Vigilence Is the Price of Efficiency;" the parody of the company play; the satire of the corporate ethos; the inflated language of the bureaucrats and managers; the *reducio ad absurdum* of the Cornell football program—there were not a lot of the "jokes" that were to become a self-described hallmark of Vonnegut's early fiction: "I am better than most people in my trade at making jokes on paper" (PS, p. 173).

Jokes for which Vonnegut became famous—or notorious—begin to appear and to proliferate in *The Sirens of Titan*, but in *Cat's Cradle* Vonnegut's mordant wit finds its appropriate subject, and the results are bitterly comic. John Leverence lists sixteen different traditional "aspects" of American humor in the novel: "the tall tale; the unreliable narrator; the Negro minstrel; comedy in a grim situation; grotesque naturalism, [sic] incongruous language; narrative objectivity in a chaotic situation; satire; anecdote; the Westerner character; alazon-eiron relationship; the yarn spinner overwhelmed by his own tale; point counter point; avoidance or deprecation of extramarital sex; the homorless narrator; sentimentality."[16] Here is an example of either "comedy in a grim situation" or "narrative objectivity in a chaotic situation"—the categories are not hard and fast—which yields grotestque humor: during an outbreak of bubonic plague, after working frantically and hopelessly without sleep for many days, Dr. Julian Castle goes from bed to bed in his hospital hoping "to find a live patient to treat," but all he finds "in bed after bed [were] . . . dead people." So he finally cracks, and taking his flashlight, he shines it on the stacks of corpses piled high outside the hospital while he says to his son: "Son, . . . someday this will all be yours" (CC, p. 112).

The joke depends upon knowing and recognizing the cliché, "Someday this will all be yours," and then putting it into the horrifying context of the plague's victims. Perhaps the best metaphor for Vonnegut's humor in *Cat's Cradle* is that of the grin on the skull beneath the skin, for in this novel, readers are never far away from death. Whichever way readers turn—politics, economics, religion or sex—they head towards death. Even when the narrator uses a harmless cliché, "It's a small world," another character replies, "When you put it in a cemetery, it is" (CC, p. 50).

The plot of *Cat's Cradle* is itself the ultimate joke in which all life on Earth perishes thanks to the greed, stupidity, and shortsightedness of that part of life called "human beings." Vonnegut was not alone in the fifties in thinking that all life on Earth was threatened. This fear of annihilation was as widespread as it appeared justified. *The Bulletin of Atomic Scientists,* a reputable journal of the period, had on its cover a Doomsday clock with the hour hand set at midnight—the time a nuclear holocaust would end "life as we know it"—while the minute hand would be adjusted on the cover of each issue to accord with the political prospects for such annihilation. For many of those years, the clock read—in a memorable book title—*Two Minutes till Midnight.* In other words, according to those scientists who should have known, life on the planet had very little time left. A famous allegorical cartoon of the time depicted a skeleton with its skull in a hideous grin as its insides were being blown up by a bomb. The thumb of its bony right hand had just pushed the plunger, activating it. Eugene O'Neill's line in *The Iceman Cometh* could stand as a motto for the times: "All things are the same meaningless joke to me, for they grin at me from the skull of death." The essential pessimism underlying this apocalyptic vision of the fifties was admirably caught in *The Fourteenth Book of Bokonon,* entitled "What Can a Thoughtful Man Hope for Mankind on Earth, Given the Experience of the Past Million Years?" As the narrator reports "It doesn't take long to read *The Fourteenth Book.* It consists of one word and a period. This is it: 'Nothing'" (CC, p. 164).

American fiction of the period included a wealth of popular novels also depicting either the end of the world or life for the remnants of humankind after an atomic holocaust. Yet few of these novels have proven as lasting as *Cat's Cradle* in large measure because Vonnegut melds his comic, satiric vision of modern society, its vacuousness and lack of purpose, with a terrifying vision of human irresponsibility and with what John May calls "our insane pretentions, both technological and religious."[17] The three Hoenikker children in *Cat's Cradle*—who have charge of the destinies of nations and, ultimately, of the whole human race—destroy all life on Earth because they do not or cannot love because they do not see themselves as part of the human community and fail to acknowledge, care, or have respect for others. Instead, they sell their horrific legacy for the usual human price of "a mess of pottage" that, in this instance, is sex, money, and power. Frank buys a generalship "just the way [Angela] . . . bought . . . a tomcat husband, just the way Newt bought himself a week on Cape Cod with a Russian midget!" (CC, p. 163). The ensuing series of accidents leads to Earth's destruction for which they are ultimately responsible. After the cataclysm, Frank says to the others with no hint of irony, "I've grown up a great deal." To which the narrator replies dryly, "At a certain amount of expense to the world" (CC, p. 187).

These "babies filled with rabies" are also Vonnegut's comment on the world's incompetent, insensitive, short-sighted leaders, thinkers, and citizens who sacrifice ultimate good for short-term and, in the last analysis, trivial gain. Having the world's destiny in their hands, as their father did before them, the Hoenikker children drop it leaving all the world and each person frozen in isolation—Vonnegut's trenchant warning on the urgent need for human community and human unity against the forces of destruction.

Opposed to this negative example of myopic greed and stupidity is the positive example of Ambassador Horlick Minton who is able to place himself and his country within the larger context of history and the world. He also sees the patriotic dead in contrast to their fellow countrymen who enjoy the precious gift of life and consciousness: those who die in wars are neither men nor martyrs but "murdered children . . . lost children . . . we might best spend the day [not in celebrating their deaths, but in] despising what killed them; which is to say, the stupidity and viciousness of all mankind" (CC, p. 170). The picture of the Mintons themselves disappearing into the Ice—those who are good, loving and part of the human community perishing because of those who are greedy and stupid and isolated—is part of what Vonnegut means by "the idea of Ice-9 had a certain moral validity . . . even though scientifically it had to be pure bunk" (WF&G, p. 97).

The notion of "Ice-9" itself came from the plot for a fantastic story that Dr. Irving Langmuir concocted to entertain H.G. Wells when the latter visited the General Electric Research Laboratory in Schenectady. Wells never used the idea, so Vonnegut said to himself, "Finders, keepers—the idea is mine." He then modelled Felix Hoenikker on Langmuir himself, the "first scientist in private industry to win a Nobel prize" (PS, p. 102).

Technically, *Cat's Cradle* ". . . best exemplies the methods and techniques of . . . [early] Vonnegut. . . . [since] almost every device, technique, attitude and subject we encounter . . . [through *Slaughter-house-Five*]" is present, as Peter Reed maintains.[18] Vonnegut's invention is at its height as he combines a satire on modern religion with one on a Banana Boat Republic's military dictatorship, and then carica-tures American greed, backslapping, good fellowship, and shortsight-edness. Like all his novels through *Slaughterhouse-Five*, *Cat's Cradle* wrestles with the very American moral problem of means and ends: does the good end ever justify employing an evil means? Rather than the schizophrenia of *Mother Night*, *Cat's Cradle* features equilibrium and balance. Johnson (Bokonon) and McCabe embrace contradictions and incorporate them into their utopia. The basis for their utopian plan is Charles Atlas's "Dynamic Tension," a method of building muscles "by simply pitting one set of muscles against another" (CC, p. 74), that "Atlas" used for his mail-order body building program familiar to most comic book readers of the forties. "It was the belief of Bokonon that good societies could be built only by pitting good against evil, and by keeping the tension between the two high at all times" (CC, p. 74). Lionel Boyd Johnson brilliantly invents his Bokononist religion and brilliantly invents himself as Bokonon both of which are "good," while Eugene McCabe creates the "bad" military dictator who will rule the island and outlaw Bokonon and Bokononism. As a result of this "tension," citizens find themselves acting in a modern morality play and "as the living legend of the cruel tyrant in the city and the gentle holy man in the jungle grew, so, too, did the happiness of the people grow. They were all employed full time as actors in a play they understood, that any human being anywhere could understand and applaud" (CC, p. 119).

Thus the potentially explosive conflict between the promise inherent in the creation of life and the threat inherent in humankind's destructive bent, which is the focus for *Cat's Cradle* as a whole, becomes reduced to "a work of art" on San Lorenzo thanks to Bokonon's foma or harmless lies which help people to live with the on-going contradictions. Bokonon sums all of this up in one of his sacred "Calypsos":

> I wanted all things
> To seem to make some sense,
> So we all could be happy, yes,
> Instead of tense.
> And I made up lies
> So that they all fit nice,
> And I made this sad world
> A par-a-dise (CC, p. 90).

Gary Wolfe contends that there is "a kind of structure for the reading of fantasy . . . which permits . . . certain fantasy works to become analogues of inner experience virtually as valid as events of the 'real world,' and which expresses the author's own most fundamental convictions."[19] The Bokononist religion appears as such a structure and is, therefore, comically serious, as the novel's plot is comically apocalyptic.

Within this plot, *Cat's Cradle* provides memorable jokes, grotesque situations, witty repartee, and clever parodies to make the very serious point that human beings can and may very well choose to end life on planet Earth. The narrator, "Jonah-John"—writing a book which he innocently believes will be about "what important Americans had done on the day when the first atomic bomb was dropped on Hiroshima, Japan" (CC, p. 11) with the working title, "The Day the World Ended"—actually ends up writing a book about the destruction of the world through Ice-9. A writer, he says, "takes on a sacred obligation to produce beauty and enlightenment and comfort at top speed" (CC, p. 156). *Cat's Cradle* is definitely "enlightening" and, as a work of imaginative literature, it has a certain "beauty," but like all of Vonnegut's early novels, it does not contain much, if any, "comfort." If anything, it appears written to "afflict the comfortable," rather than bring comfort to the afflicted. While other commentators were enthusiastic about the possibilities of technology solving the great problems of war, waste, illness and poverty, Vonnegut remained skeptical, and in *Cat's Cradle* downright fearful.[20] With the passing decades, more and more thinkers, scientists, and social commentators have allied themselves with his view until, at the end of the eighties, those in the fifties and sixties who announced that they believed in progress through technology now appear quaintly irrelevant to the problems facing the world.

Cat's Cradle remains Vonnegut's comic masterpiece and, together with *Slaughterhouse-Five* and *Bluebeard,* his best work to date. This memorable book has worn well over the twenty-five or more years since its publication, and most readers will concur with Vonnegut's own evaluation of it as the best of the five early novels. Within the book, the comedy spares no one: from the narrow military mind and values, to the scientist's lack of morality and vision to the hypocrisy of religion to the dedicated American's will to get-ahead to the Hossier *granfaloon.* The telegraphese style with its short punchy sentences and hilarious chapter titles (developed further from *The Sirens of Titan*) proves an exact match for his subject. The invented *Books of Bokonon* form a moral core for the novel that Vonnegut uses to comment on or provide counterpoint to the action. Bokonon, along with John, the naive narrator, helps establish the positive set of values—in an otherwise mad whirling world—so necessary for the success of this apocalyptic satire. These positive values include a belief in the sanctity of human beings, the necessity for human love, the primacy of human community, and the vision of a world larger than a single person, family, or country.

The Uselessness of Human Beings
God Bless You, Mr. Rosewater or Pearls Before Swine

At the center of *God Bless You, Mr. Rosewater* lie the Great Depression and World War II: two overwhelming experiences that left their mark on its hero, Eliot Rosewater, as well as on all those around him. Brought up to believe that God blesses those who truly believe and work hard, Americans found themselves in the Great Depression with no work, with no means to support their families, and, therefore, with no value: no jobs, no income, no worth—a simple but devastating equation. Tossed aside by society, like so many empty husks, men began wandering across the country—useless men with no jobs, no families, no one to care for and no one to care for them. The legacy, for Vonnegut's generation, was devastating. And so he concludes that "part of the trick for people my age, I'm certain, is to crawl out of the envying, life-hating mood of the Great Depression at last" (WF&G, p. 285).

Eliot Rosewater overcomes this "envying, life-hating mood" in his life, then works to help others overcome it in theirs. The people he helps are those society judges as "useless," much like those who were battered by the Great Depression. Near the end of the novel in answer to his father, Senator Rosewater's contention that "A poor man with gumption can still elevate himself out of the mire . . . and that will continue to be true a thousand years from now," Kilgore Trout asserts that "Poverty is a relatively mild disease for even a very flimsy American soul, but uselessness will kill strong and weak souls alike, and kill every time" (GB, p. 184). This is as close as any character in *God Bless You, Mr. Rosewater* or any of the early novels comes to preaching, but undercutting the sentiment is the character of the preacher himself: for the words are put into the mouth of Trout, the hack science-fiction writer who works at a stamp redemption center! (Some critics of Vonnegut become so preoccupied with Kilgore Trout that they attach more importance to him than his actual place in this particular novel deserves. Later, he will become a major character in *Slaughterhouse-Five, Breakfast of Champions,* and *Jailbird,* while making an appearance in *Galápagos.* Here, he is an amusing minor character who, first, shows Eliot's limitations as a reader—he reads only for plot since, as he says, "writers [such as Trout] couldn't write for sour apples" [GB, p. 18]—and, second, through his fiction Trout does for readers what Eliot attempts to do with his money which is to provide people "with fantasies of an impossibly hospitable world" [GB, p. 20]. Finally at the end of the novel, Trout is brought onstage to give his sermon on the dangers of soul-rot and the uselessness of human beings.)

Eliot tries to overcome his and others' feeling of uselessness by giving them "uncritical love" and by attempting to do "good works" both large and small.[21] His life comes to reflect the Sermon on the Mount (Matthew 5-6) in that he becomes one of the "meek," who, Jesus says, will inherit not riches, such as the Rosewater fortune, but "the earth"—his true inheritance. Knowing that it is harder for a rich man to enter heaven than for a camel to pass through the eye of a needle, he stops being a "rich man" and becomes poorer than the poor. Although disuaded by lawyers from selling all he has and giving it to the poor—as Jesus admonished the young rich man to do—in the end he does manage to distribute his fortune to innocent strangers. In another memorable sermon, Jesus divides people into those who do such good works and those who do not; between those who "when I was an hungred . . . gave me meat; I was thirsty . . . gave me drink; I was a stranger, . . . took me in; Naked and . . . clothed me; . . . sick and . . . visited me: . . . in prison, and . . . came unto me. Then shall the righteous answer him, saying, Lord, when saw we *thee* an hungred, and fed *thee*? or thirsty, and gave *thee* drink? . . . And [He] the King shall answer and say unto them. Verily I say unto you, In as much as ye have done *it* unto one of the least of these my brethren, ye have done *it* unto me" (Matthew 25:35-40).

Eliot visits the sick, comforts the lonely, feeds the hungry, and gives drink to the thirsty. He helps others through the Volunteer Fire Department. He is the one who listens to those who have no listener, who visits those in the prison of themselves, and those who are the outcasts of society. As Diana Moon Glampers tells him at the end of a telephone conversation in the middle of the night when Eliot treats her like a human being, taking her fears seriously, with never a trace of sarcasm: "You gave up everything a man is supposed to want, just to help the little people, and the little people know it. God bless you, Mr. Rosewater" (GB, p. 61).

In addition, Eliot realizes that money's prime function in philanthropy lies in its symbolic value, which shows that someone cares. His beautiful wife divorces him not because she hates what he does or because she does not approve or understand, but because she does not have the stamina to keep on doing it with him (GB, p. 53-54). It takes huge quantities of emotional energy to "[treasure] human beings because they are human beings" (GB, p. 183), which is what Eliot is attempting to do. A typical caller to the Rosewater Foundation will begin talking to him by saying "I'm nothing" (GB, p. 74) and believing it. Realizing that wealth will not help such folk, nor the "arts and sciences," he invents things for them to do which will fill up their time, such as fly hunts; he offers them his prescription against most minor aches and pains both physical and emotional, "take an aspirin with a glass of wine," and he keeps laxatives handy for most other complaints.

Although "people can use all the uncritical love they can get" (GB, p. 186), many have a vested interest in seeing that people do not receive it. One of those is the unscrupulous young lawyer, Norman Mushari, who is determined to rid Eliot of his fortune and in the process siphon off a sizable chunk of it into his own safekeeping. Eliot's response to his attack is to refuse to do battle, to refuse to fight by hiring other lawyers. Rather than making an opposing argument in court, he "turns the other cheek" by giving away his fortune through inheriting the fifty-seven or more children who claim him as their father. Hence, the Rosewater fortune, which is a "leading character" in the book, leaves the Rosewater family forever, never to burden another with the responsibility of caring for it. No wonder Eliot feels relieved and happy at the end. His last words echo God's to his new creations, the Man and Woman in the Garden of Eden: "Be fruitful and multiply." Like God in the Bible, either in the Old Testament (See Hosea) or the New Testament (See Roman's and the Sermon on the Mount), Eliot uses formal, sacramental language to assure his children of his uncritical, forgiving love: "Let their names be Rosewater from this moment on. And tell them that their father loves them, no matter what they may turn out to be" (GB, p. 190). Clearly the way to overcome envy and "life-hating"—at least in this novel—is to love.

The other significant event influencing the novel's values and action is World War II, which, in the United States, appeared to eliminate ambiguity from national and private morality because the enemy was portrayed as so terrible, so inhuman, so evil. But moral ambiguity resurfaced when those who participated in the war, such as Eliot, found themselves in predicaments that forced them to ask difficult questions about their own or their country's actions. As discussed earlier, for Vonnegut, these questions usually focus on the Allies' bombing the "open," undefended city of Dresden where the resulting firestorm incinerated 135,000 people within a few hours. Such actions led to an ethical dilemma: what happens if the "good" side uses inhuman, evil means (fire storms in Dresden or the atomic bomb on Hiroshima or Nagasaki) to achieve a good end (the defeat of Germany and Japan)? Is the result good or evil? Or is it perhaps morally neutral? These questions were part of what was earlier described as the "moral hangover" left by the war.

In *God Bless You, Mr. Rosewater*, the "hangover" is appallingly present in Eliot Rosewater's terrible memory of the disaster, which occurred when he did his duty and obeyed what appeared to be legitimate orders given "under fire." He had been told to take an objective and hold it. So he heroically led his troops in an assault on a building and personally killed three men before someone realized that the enemy were unarmed, and, worse, were firemen "engaged in the brave and uncontroversial business of trying to keep a building from combining with oxygen" (GB, p. 64). To make matters even worse, Eliot discovers that, of his three unarmed victims, the two he killed with a grenade were old men, while the one he bayonetted was a teenage boy! So it goes. It was, of course, no one's fault—"mistakes" are bound to happen in war, but Eliot now has to live the rest of his life with the memory of killing three unarmed people who were acting selflessly to save the property and lives of others. Vonnegut uses him as a living microcosm for studying some of the moral questions posed by the macrocosm of World War II where, as he and other writers— most notably Joseph Heller in *Catch-22*—have pointed out, not everything was as morally clear-cut as American propaganda made it out to be.

Vonnegut avoids treating either this ghastly "mistake" or the many instances of Eliot's "good deeds" with sentimentality—always a danger in a novel with a "good hero"—in part by showing his main character's considerable limitations both in themselves and in contrast with those of other characters. Eliot dramatically contrasts with Henry Pena, for example, the robust, healthy fisherman who with his sons works hard for a living, is in constant danger of bankruptcy, and maintains a clear sense of what is "real" and what is unreal, fantasy or phoney whether it is a fish, woman or man. Eliot enjoys none of these positive virtues, attributes, or abilities. Instead, he is alcoholic, fat, mentally disturbed and suffers from a bad conscience. Yet he does what he can to alleviate pain and suffering in the little town of Rosewater, Indiana, while his unknown nemesis, Mushari, plots to steal his inherited fortune by proving him mentally incompetent. (His father also emphasizes his son's limits when he hires a psychiatrist who says Eliot is bringing his sexual energies "to Utopia" and "has the potential for a samaritrophic collapse" [GB, pp. 73, 43]). Eliot, himself, helps dampen sanctimony by comically reducing the radical thrust of Christianity's New Commandment that "you love your enemies, bless them that curse you, do good to them that hate you, and pray for them which despitefully use you, and persecute you . . ." (Matthew 5:44) to "'God damn it, you've got to be kind'" (GB, p. 93).

Unlike the evil Campbell in *Mother Night,* Eliot is clearly a good person. In many ways, he is as naive as Paul Proteus in *Player Piano,* as misguided as Constant in *The Sirens of Titan,* and as removed as Jonah-John in *Cat's Cradle.* His behavior, while judged "insane" or at least highly eccentric by others in positions of power or responsibility, is, when looked at in light of Vonnegut's ethics, eminently sane and highly commendible. Although Vonnegut is a rational atheist who clearly rejects all forms of institutional religion (WF&G, p. 240), in this novel he appears to advocate what might be loosely described as "Christian ethics" based upon the Sermon on the Mount in which Jesus admonished his listeners to follow a discipline of radical love, even to loving one's enemies and "doing good to them that hate you."

One of Vonnegut's best stories about his early life in Indianapolis illustrates the power of these New Testament texts. In it, he tells of a luncheon meeting between his father, a wealthy, successful architect whose fortune was wiped out in the Great Depression, who was by this time "in full retreat from life" (*Jailbird,* p. 13); his Uncle Alex, who was puzzled by, though sympathetic with, his young nephew; and Powers Hapgood, the Harvard educated labor organizer. Hapgood arrived straight from the court where he was "testifying about violence on a picket line some months before. . . . The judge was fascinated . . . 'Mr. Hapgood,' he said, 'why would a man from such a distinguished family and with such a fine education choose to live as you do?' 'Why?' said Hapgood, . . . 'Because of the Sermon on the Mount, sir.'" Apparently unable to frame an appropriate reply, the judge declared a recess (*Jailbird,* pp. 18-19).

At the end of *God Bless You, Mr. Rosewater,* Eliot's hard won victory may prove ephemeral, for while he believes he has found a

54

solution "for settling everything instantly, beautifully, and fairly" (GB, p. 188) in giving his inheritance away, the world in which he lives will view it as "crazy." His three criteria, "instantly, beautifully and fairly," are naively utopian, although perfectly consistent with his life—as contrasted with his father's and grandfather's. Readers surely hope that having so quickly cut the Gordian Knot created by Mushari, he will be able to return to peaceful Rosewater County, Indiana, and take up his old life, but judging from earlier events, his prospects may not be that good. When the greedy lawyer forces him to leave Rosewater to defend his way of life, he becomes catatonic. Subsequently, he has a vision of the destruction of the Earth in a firestorm, similar to the one which destroyed Dresden, in which he sees the firestorm directly over Indianapolis "at least eight miles in diameter and fifty miles high" (GB, p. 176). (In much the same way his own world of Rosewater County at that moment appears about to be destroyed by lawyers, courts, and what the world calls "obligations.") Eliot's efforts may, therefore, be doomed, for as Clark Mayo contends: "*God Bless You, Mr. Rosewater* deals with the confusions of money, power and love in a 'Free Enterprise System,'" which provides a hostile environment for "uncritical love" in mid-twentieth century America.[22] At the end of the novel, readers are left with the question of which will prevail: Eliot's plan for fairness and beauty or the firestorm of destruction and greed?

It is difficult to place *God Bless You, Mr. Rosewater* or these early novels as a group comfortably within any scheme, although many have tried. Various novels have been labelled alternately: science-fiction, black humor, satire, schizophrenic, fabulation, and fantasy. While there is some truth in each of these labels, depending upon which novel or group of novels one reads and from which perspective, the important truth is that Vonnegut's work escapes such easy classification. He has written successful science-fiction, as he has some black humor; he definitely is a satirist and he surely is a fantastist, but each of his novels is unique. *God Bless You, Mr. Rosewater*, for instance, differs from the other early novels in that its form is highly traditional and those parts which are truly fantastic are incorporated as Kilgore Trout science–fiction novels and stories—a device which will become a staple of Vonnegut's later fiction.[23] Unlike the other novels, its hero, although in an insane asylum, is neither dead nor facing death at the end and has some hope of at least frustrating, if not overcoming, the evil and stupid forces arrayed against him.

What can be clearly seen already in the five novels preceding *Slaughterhouse-Five* is Vonnegut's willingness to tackle major moral, social, and political issues from genocide to automation, from the significance or lack of it in history, to the possible end of the world. He also examines contemporary evil in the schizophrenic mentality of the double agent or of those who developed and deployed the Bomb, and of those who invented and staffed the death camps. He warns against valuing automation as better than human variety and inefficency and against evaluating people by their uniforms of race, color, creed or nationality rather than by their flesh and blood human desires and needs. Finally, he rejects the discarding of some of humanity as useless and unworthy of love. Juxtaposed to these negative values is Vonnegut's positive vision of the fragility and worth of each human being and of the need "to love whoever is around to be loved."

Arthur Koestler might have been describing the future course and subjects of Vonnegut's novels when he wrote:

> Electronic brains . . ., lie detectors . . ., new drugs . . ., radiations . . .—all these developments of the past fifty years have created new vistas and new nightmares which art and literature have not yet assimilated. In a crude and fumbling fashion, science fiction is trying to fill this gap.[24]

Vonnegut did assimilate "these developments" along with many others which Koestler failed to mention, such as automation, genocide, the Bomb, philanthropy, the meaning or lack of it in history, and, especially, the need for an alert, creative consciousness. He did so without "fumbling" but with considerable artistic skill: writing science-fiction in *The Sirens of Titan* and *Cat's Cradle*, dystopian fiction in *Player Piano*, historical fiction in *Mother Night*, and traditional fiction in *God Bless You, Mr. Rosewater*. In these novels, Vonnegut challenges the reader to examine how he or she acts, thinks or feels which, as Richard Poirier reminds us, is the most important task of the writer: "We do not go to literature to become better citizens or even wiser persons, but to discover how to move, to act, to work in ways that are still and forever mysteriously creative."[25]

NOTES

1 Robert Scholes, "A Talk with Kurt Vonnegut, Jr.," in *The Vonnegut Statement*, ed. Jerome Klinkowitz and John Somer (New York: Dell, 1973), pp. 93-94.

2 Charlie Reilly, "Two Conversations with Kurt Vonnegut," *College Literature*, 7.1 (Winter 1980), p. 3.

3 Ibid., p. 4.

4 Ibid.; compare: WF&G, p. 261.

5 "Ironic Historicism in the American Novel of the Sixties," *John O'Hara Journal* 5.1&2 (Winter 1982-83), p. 87.

6 *The Abandoned Snail Shell* (Dublin: The Raven Arts Press, 1987), p. 19.

7 G.K. Wolfe, "Vonnegut and the Metaphor of Science Fiction: The Sirens of Titan [sic]," *Journal of Popular Culture*, 4 (Spring 1972), p. 968.

8 *Pilgrim's Progress* (New York: Holt, Rinehart and Winston, 1949), p. 11.

9 *Vonnegut: A Preface to His Novels* (Port Washington: Kennikat Press, 1977), p. 37.

10 According to Vonnegut, his model for Rumfoord was President Franklin Delano Roosevelt. In response to a question about what analogies there might be "between what Rumfoord does in the novel and . . . what Roosevelt did socially and politically . . .," Vonnegut said: "They both have enormous hope for changing things . . . childish hopes, too. I don't think Roosevelt was an enormous success except as a personality." "Interview" with John Casey and Joe David Bellamy in *The New Fiction: Interviews with Innovative American Writers*, ed. Joe David Bellamy (Urbana: University of Illinois Press, 1974), p. 199.

11 Wolfe, (See note 7), p. 969.

12 Vonnegut gives his source of inspiration for *Mother Night* as a cocktail party conversation he had with an ex-Intelligence officer who maintained that all spies "are schizophrenics. They have to be insane . . . because otherwise they would either blow their covers or simply die of fright... someone ought to make a spy movie about what spies are really like. So I wrote a book about it." Reilly, op. cit., p. 8. Vonnegut's account weakens somewhat Tony Tanner's suggestion: " . . . that the book may well have been inspired by the case of Ezra Pound . . . in 1960 Charles Norman's biography appeared. This contained the . . . information that apparently the Italian Government 'mistrusted the broadcasts, even suspecting that they hid a code language.'" *The City of Words: American Fiction, 1950-1970* (London: Jonathan Cape, 1971), pp. 186-87.

13 Rosemary Jackson maintains that "Dialogues of self and other are increasingly acknowledged as being colloquies with the self: any demonic presences are generated from within." *Fantasy: the Literature of Subversion* (New York: Methuen, 1981), p. 108. Vonnegut wrote plays based upon the plot of *Dr. Jekyll and Mr. Hyde* and the character of Frankenstein; "The Chemistry Professor-treatment by KV for a musical comedy based on Stevenson's Dr. Jekyll and Mr. Hyde" (PS, pp. 260-290), while "Fortitude" features a modern-day Dr. Norbert Frankenstein and his "enthusiastic first assistant," Dr. Tom Swift (WF&G, pp. 43-64).

14 Reilly (See note 2), 24.

15 Robert Scholes, "A Talk with Kurt Vonnegut, Jr." in *The Vonnegut Statement* ed. Jerome Klinkowitz and John Somer (New York: Dell), 1973, p. 115.

16 *"Cat's Cradle* and Traditional American Humor," *Journal of Popular Culture,* 5 (Spring 1972), p. 955.

17 *Toward a New Earth: Apocalypse in the American Novel* (Notre Dame: University Press of Notre Dame, 1972), p. 200.

18 *Kurt Vonnegut, Jr.* (New York: Crowell, 1972), p. 119.

19 "The Encounter with Fantasy," *The Aesthetics of Fantasy Literature and Art,* ed. Roger C. Schlobin (Notre Dame: University of Notre Dame Press, 1982), p. 13.

20 See: "Excelsior! We're Going to the Moon! Excelsior!" WF&G, pp. 77-89).

21 Vonnegut once shared an office with the man who became his model for Eliot Rosewater: "... there really is a man who is that *kind.* Except he's poor, an accountant over a liquor store. We shared an office, and I could hear him comforting people who had very little income, calling everybody 'dear' and giving love and understanding instead of money. ... I took this very sweet man and in a book gave him millions and millions to play with." Interview with John Casey et al, op cit., p. 199. Giannone suggests that "Rosewater seems modelled after his nineteenth century namesake Frank Rosewater who in 1894 wrote *'96: A Romance of Utopia: Presenting a Solution of the Labor Problem, a New God and a New Religion,"* but offers no evidence other than the suggestive book title ("Violence in the Fiction of Kurt Vonnegut." *Thought* 56.220 (March 1981), p. 64).

22 *Kurt Vonnegut: The Gospel from Outer Space* (San Bernardino: Borgo, 1977), p. 37.

23 See especially: Kathryn Hume,"Vonnegut's Self- Projections: Symbolic Characters and Symbolic Fiction," *The Journal of Narrative Technique,* 12 (Fall 1982), pp. 177-90.

24 "The Boredom of Fantasy." *Harper's Bazaar,* August 1953, p. 122.

25 *The Renewal of Literature: Emersonian Reflections* (New Haven: Yale University Press, 1987), p. 44.

V. Vonnegut at Play
Breakfast of Champions, Slapstick,
Happy Birthday, Wanda June,
Between Time and Timbuktu or Prometheus-5

After the enormous popular and critical success of *Slaughter-house-Five,* Vonnegut declared that he was going to turn away from fiction to try playwrighting and so spent most of 1970-71 writing and rewriting *Happy Birthday, Wanda June,* which opened in New York on October 7, 1970, and ran for 142 performances until March 14, 1971. Besides this quite respectable run for a first play, Vonnegut also enjoyed kind reviews and several good interviews. Clive Barnes concluded his review for *The New York Times*: "Mr. Vonnegut has not written much of a play, but he has provided a decently, sometimes indecently, diverting evening."[1] In addition to being his first relatively successful venture into commercial theatre, the play also becomes part of his personal search for community, a search made even clearer in the post-catastrophic utopian fantasy, *Slapstick* (1976).

A day short of a year after the play closed, Vonnegut had a ninety-minute television special, *Between Time and Timbuktu,* on the Public Broadcasting Service network that proved to be a great delight for him: ". . . I told other writers, 'Hey, get into non-commercial television'" (TT, p. xiv). The program was every comic writer's dream: a ninety-minute TV special of your own works with Bob and Ray as co-anchors! "When Bob Elliot and Ray Goulding agreed to work on this TV show," says Vonnegut, "I nearly swooned. I would have been less in awe of Winston Churchill and Charles de Gaulle" (TT, p. xvii). Meanwhile, the film version of *Slaughterhouse-Five,* released in 1972, proved an artistic, commercial, and critical success. There was talk and even an option to produce a musical version of one or another of his novels, and Vonnegut himself, in 1970, after describing a new play he was working on about "a woman pornographer" predicted, "If I live to be 65 or 70 I will have written 10 novels and six plays."[2] But all of this flirtation with film, television, and the stage proved temporary, and in 1972 in the preface to *Between Time and Timbuktu,* Vonnegut announced his return to writing novels and for a very special reason—one that is central to the success or failure of his fiction through *Slapstick*:

I have become an enthusiast for the printed word again. I have to be that, I now understand, because I want to be a character in all of my works. I can do that in print. In a movie, somehow, the author always vanishes (TT, p. xv).

So in his next published novel, *Breakfast of Champions* (1979), which he calls, "my fiftieth birthday present to myself" (BC, p. 4), he is very much in evidence as the narrator and character. Curiously, Vonnegut has said that ". . . *Slaughterhouse* and *Breakfast* used to be one book. But they just separated completely. . . . I was able to decant *Slaughterhouse-Five*, and what was left was *Breakfast of Champions*" (WF&G, p. 281). Some readers see this book as clear evidence of Vonnegut's being mentally and emotionally drained by the efforts required to write *Slaughterhouse-Five,* and many critics have viewed the rest of his work as a descent from the peak of Billy Pilgrim's story, but such is really not the case. Rather, after dealing with such large, imponderable issues as the presence of evil in the world and unmotivated human suffering, Vonnegut turns to "playing" in a serious way with the nature of narrative and with his role as a writer which results in the wonderful exuberance of *Breakfast of Champions.*

Entering his fifties, Vonnegut found that one phase of his life appeared to be over, while another was apparently "powerless to be born": his marriage had fallen apart, his children had left home and no longer needed him, he had renounced fiction in favor of writing drama, and he had tried commuting to teach at Harvard, then moved alone to New York City. Like many people at his age, he found himself in a time of waiting—waiting for whatever would happen next. He also knew the blackness of separation from family and friends: "...the story of an American father's departure from his hearth . . . , in my opinion, is a tale of a man's cold sober flight into unpopulated nothingness" (PS, p. 304). In a small apartment in New York City, he found truth in a Statler Brothers' song, "Flowers on the Wall," which he calls, "another great contemporary poem" and quotes in a personally revealing essay, "The Sexual Revolution." Vonnegut's comments on the song tell volumes about his feelings at that time: "It is not a poem of escape or rebirth. It is a poem about the end of a man's usefulness" (PS, pp. 305, 307).

This may be, in part, what Vonnegut means when he describes *Breakfast of Champions* as his wrestling with the question of suicide. He concludes that *"Breakfast of Champions* isn't a threat to commit suicide, incidentally. It's my promise that I'm beyond that now. Which is something for me" (WF&G, p. 283). Psychologists believe that suicide is more of a positive choice for children of suicides than for most other people. Vonnegut, whose mother committed suicide in 1944, is aware of this pressure. (For his discussion of "Sons of suicides seldom do well," see GB, p. 103.) But there is also the metaphoric suicide of the writer who despairs over ever writing again. Here, also, *Breakfast of Champions* suggests that Vonnegut is past that point, that he can return to writing as "a very pleasant endeavor,"[3] that he has dealt with the extreme pain occasioned by his children leaving and by his separation and subsequent divorce. "It is hard to adapt to chaos," he says in *Breakfast of Champions*, "but it can be done. I am living proof of that: It can be done" (BC, p. 210). In other words, he has come through what Carl Jung called "the mid-life crisis" when people must decide what they will do next with their lives. Whether a person succeeds, fails, or simply survives the early years, he or she must then decide what to do for whatever remains of his or her active working life. Vonnegut credits writing with actually saving his life during this terribly painful experience (PS, p. 322). He decides to continue writing and to write about what he knows well from his own experience: the terrible self-destructive bent of human beings, the necessity for establishing some form of viable human community, and the process of rebirth and rejoining humanity. As the reborn hero of *Slapstick* predicts, when people ". . . 'experience . . . companionship . . . [it] allow[s] them to climb the evolutionary ladder [and] . . . become human beings, after having been for so many years . . . centipedes and slugs and earwigs and worms'" (SS, p. 177).

In *Breakfast of Champions*, he parodies the "crisis" he experienced by writing about becoming fifty years old as if that moment would suddenly demarcate a line of great significance by dividing the years behind from those ahead, as well as his two major decisions—both later recanted—to stop writing fiction and to create only new characters, rather than bringing back old ones. The work reflects a secure as well as mature writer, one who feels free to experiment with

61

narration and even, surprisingly, with magic marker drawings, as it is also the work of a highly successful writer whose publisher willingly indulges him by agreeing to publish whatever he writes. Perhaps "antic novel" is the best descriptive term for *Breakfast of Champions*. For it is a marvelous melange of familiar characters, plots, and jokes, told in a short punchy style with Kurt Vonnegut, himself, in a central role as narrator.

Vonnegut once said, in response to a question in a televised interview, "If you make things move fast enough, you can say anything. . . . and I am trying to be a good citizen."[4] In *Breakfast of Champions*, he successfully mixes serious social and political commentary with antic action. One of the results is an entertaining, yet still very serious warning against the effects of pollution, commercial exploitation, war, racism, and, above all, drug dependency and addiction. For example, he savagely and satirically attacks white racism through the gruesome story Dwayne Hoover's father tells of a lynch mob sawing an innocent man "in two on the top strand of a barbed-wire fence" (BC, p. 240), which he recounts with approval to his son as together they dump garbage and trash into Sugar Creek, thus adding ecological pollution to their emotional and verbal pollution.

The novel's style is disengenuously naive as Vonnegut, as narrator, writes as if to someone from another planet who is totally unfamiliar with Earth and Earthlings' strange ways, especially those of people living on that part of the planet called the United States of America. The result is a form of comic dislocation as he describes with an absolutely straight face what is happening to and in the America of the 1970's. Here, for example, is the description of Kilgore Trout hitching a ride from New York City to Midland City:

> He crossed the island of Manhattan from east to west in the company of Kleenex tissues and newspapers and soot.
>
> He got a ride on a truck. It was hauling seventy-eight thousand pounds of Spanish olives. It picked him up at the mouth of the Lincoln Tunnel, which was named in honor of a man who had had the courage and imagination to make human slavery against the law in the United States of America. This was a recent innovation.

The slaves were simply turned loose without any property. They were easily recognizable. They were black. They were suddenly free to go exploring (BC, p. 83).

Of the nine sentences quoted, eight are simple declarative sentences—subject, verb, object—and very few of the words have more than two syllables. It is as if the narrator is explaining something to a child. What he is explaining, of course, is neither more nor less than the origins and continuation of America's racism, with its failure to provide for the newly freed slaves, its failure to offer work and opportunities to black people. The second thing he explains is America's willingness to despoil the planet to manufacture waste, "Kleenex tissues, and newspapers and soot" or "wash day products, catfood, pop," all of which result in the "poisoned marshes and meadows of New Jersey" through which the truck rolls (BC, p. 84). Again the narrator, as if explaining to someone on another planet, comments on the truck driver's regret: "It broke his heart when he imagined what the marshes and meadows had been like only a hundred years before. . . . He had a point. The planet was being destroyed by manufacturing processes, and what was being manufactured was lousy, by and large" (BC, p. 84). Later the driver perceptively remarks that "he knew that his truck was turning the atmosphere into poison gas, and that the planet was being turned into pavement so his truck could go anywhere. 'So I'm committing suicide,' he said" (BC, p. 85). A third satiric target, which the simplicity and logic of the narrator help hit, is war. The narrator, for example, explains the logic behind the Vietnam war to his nonterrestial audience: "Viet Nam was a country where America was trying to make people stop being communists by dropping things on them from airplanes. The chemicals . . . were intended to kill all the foliage, so it would be harder for communists to hide from airplanes" (BC, pp. 85-86). The notion of changing a people's political beliefs "by dropping things on them from airplanes" is worthy of a Jonathan Swift or a Mark Twain. Here is logic gone haywire where the means used almost guarantee that the end they were designed to achieve will not be reached. People who are being bombed rarely regard the bombers as friends nor do they see the bombing as part of an educative or pursuasive process but as designed solely for their destruction. The satire and comedy work by taking the political and moral justification for the Vietnam War, saving that part of the world from communism, and juxtaposing it to the means used, bombs and, worse, napalm and defoliants. The naive style, and the pose of the innocent, objective, uninvolved narrator—"I just got here myself," might sum up his attitude—work beautifully to point out the lunacy of manufacturing poisons and deliberately destroying the planet to "save" it from anything!

This narrator is both entertaining and informative with an indiscriminate interest in everything on this strange planet. In fact, the novel is filled with miscellaneous odd bits and pieces of information, such as the "Archetechtonic Plate Theory" of the Earth (BC, p. 143), the identity and biography of St. Anthony (BC, pp. 211-212), the diagram of a plastic molecule (BC, p. 227), the famous Nelson Rockefeller greeting and handshake, and the description of "a Mexican beetle which could make a blankcartridge gun out of its rear end. It could detonate its own farts and knock over other bugs with shock waves" (BC, p. 160). Here is a deadpan always-willing-to-explain-even-the-obvious narrator whose pose reflects his objectivity, while emphasizing how removed he is from the action.

Another of Vonnegut's fictional techniques, which enhances his satire and comedy, is his invented, failed, science–fiction writer, Kilgore Trout. Trout is a failure in every sense of that word, not just in one or two: he is a failure commercially, being published in sleezy porn magazines as filler between the lurid, graphic pictures; he is a failure critically, having never been reviewed or acknowledged by any reader, reviewer or critic, except Eliot Rosewater who has enough money to make Trout famous; and he is a failure artistically, producing only hack work, trivia, and ill-considered potboilers. (All of which makes him a perfect foil for Vonnegut's own work which is carefully formed and crafted.) He is also a sort of alter-ego for Vonnegut in that, for most of his early career until *Slaughterhouse-Five*, Vonnegut went largely unreviewed and unnoticed. (Two of his novels were paperback originals because publishers had confined him to the "drawer" of science-fiction writers [WF&G, pp. 1-5]; and several were never reviewed until after he became a success.) It may very well be true, as some observors have suggested, that the time when Vonnegut began to take himself seriously as a writer was when, at the University of Iowa, he discovered that his works were the object of serious study by serious people.[5]

In *Breakfast of Champions*, as in other novels, Kilgore Trout spins improbable and half-thought out plots that allow Vonnegut to introduce ideas, motifs, characters, and situations without committing himself to them fictionally or having to make them part of the story. Trout also has a key role in the climax of the story when Vonnegut, as narrator, makes his long-awaited announcement about setting his characters "free." He does so by confronting Trout as his creator, but Trout in turn uses the opportunity to make his own request:

> "I am approaching my fiftieth birthday, Mr. Trout," I said. "I am cleansing and renewing myself for the very different sorts of years to come. Under similar spiritual conditions, Count Tolstoi freed his serfs. Thomas Jefferson freed his slaves. I am going to set at liberty all the literary characters who have served me so loyally during my writing career" (BC, p. 293).

And Trout, who as the novel progresses has come more and more to resemble Vonnegut's father, answers in a voice that is also that of Vonnegut's father, *"Make me young, make me young, make me young!"* (BC, p. 295). Trout dreams of returning to his youth, dreams of magically receiving a second chance from his creator—as do many people, but with the difference that this creator, as a novelist, can make such fantasies come true by simply typing a new page. Yet even here, there is an ironic joke at Trout's expense, for he makes the mistake of asking for youth and no more, and Vonnegut, as his creator, willingly obliges him and in *Jailbird* (1979), grants his wish and makes him younger but at the same time places him in jail serving a life sentence! As the Latin satirist said, "When the gods want to punish us, they answer our prayers!"

Breakfast of Champions itself is much like Trout's wish: a fantasy of returning to lost innocence. Set in the bleak landscape of New York City, then in the psychotically disturbed one of Midland City, the book maintains an innocence throughout even when discussing pornography, pollution, and crime. In part, this viewpoint is achieved by the narrator's ability to treat everything and everyone equally so that nothing surprises and nothing stands out—not even himself as creator. As a creator, the narrator is not personally remarkable: yes, he can leap a huge car with a "single bound," but meanwhile one of his characters breaks his toe, and a dog from another version of the novel almost bites him! Not exactly an outstanding record. Yes, he can foretell the future, but whatever he says is truly trivial and ultimately not very revealing. Seemingly unable to really manipulate his characters, he discovers that once he creates them they have lives of their own that he cannot violate.

Behind *Breakfast of Champions* and its plot lies another dream of regaining the lost innocence of the United States, which was once a green and pleasant land, but is now in great danger of being destroyed by greed, lust, and stupidity. Where is the promise of America, "the last and greatest of all human dreams," as Fitzgerald puts it in *The Great Gatsby?* Gone on the Interstate, gone in the motel, gone in the polluting washing powder and tissues and waste. Where is the dream of the young child staring at the cereal box with its motto, "Breakfast of Champions," which promises that she, too, can be a winner, a "champion?" Gone in trivia, gone in consumerism. And in its place, the pornographic dream of male dominance parodied in *Breakfast of Champions* by the significantly large dimensions of the narrator's penis.

Here is a book in which the author describes himself as "having ascended one slope" of a roof, he now finds himself "crossing the spine" (BC, p. 4). The "dance with death" of *Slaughterhouse-Five* is still present in the discussion and option of suicide (BC, p. 192) and in the certain knowledge all the characters and the narrator have of mortality, but here it is linked with the book's antic comedy and playfulness. In *Breakfast of Champions*, Vonnegut shares with his reader the exhilaration that comes with "crossing the spine" with the attendant danger of being so far above the ground, along with the spectacular view which the height gives of the human comedy. Resisting "the seduction of fatalism," he suggests, as Robert Merrill says, that if "we cannot make ourselves young again, . . . we can make ourselves more humane."[6]

In contrast, no one would ever describe the author or the narrator of *Slapstick* as "crossing the spine of a roof." Rather *Slapstick* appears more a book of waiting—Vonnegut waiting for inspiration and viable plots, waiting to ascertain the future direction of his life and fiction. Gone is the exuberance of *Breakfast of Champions* and missing is the frenetic activity of *The Sirens of Titan*. In their place is the "day-dream" Vonnegut has as he flies to his uncle's funeral and meditates on the loss of his sister to cancer several years before:

> It would have been catastrophic if I had forgotten my sister at once. I had never told her so, but she was the person I had always written for. She was the secret of whatever artistic unity I had ever achieved. She was the secret of my technique (SS, p. 15).

Slapstick is a novel of a tired person, one worn down a bit by events, by the trials and tragedies of human life, one who is "experiment[ing] with old age" (SS, p. 19). Even its moral tag sounds tired, though it is admittedly famous: "If you can do no good, at least do no harm" (Hypocrites, SS, p. 141). The book also shows the danger for Vonnegut in dismissing Kilgore Trout, as he did in *Breakfast of Champions*, for he really needs the failed hack writer to wash out some of the unrealized parts of the plot. Still, the book remains Vonnegut's very real cry against the loneliness that almost all Americans experience, and his assertion that there is little or no comfort to be found in traditional religion nor any consolation to be derived from traditional notions of an After Life. Religion and a belief in an After Life are satirically treated in "The Church of Jesus Christ the Kidnapped . . . destined to become the most popular American religion of all time." His description of the believers is comic, "He was jerking his head around in what . . . seemed an eccentric manner, as though hoping to catch someone peering out at him from behind a potted palm tree or an easy chair, or even from directly overhead, from the crystal chandelier [in the hotel]" (SS, p. 184), but the satiric edge, so much in evidence in The Church of God the Utterly Indifferent (ST) or in the religion of Bokonon (CC), is gone. In its place appears only amusement at the comic action of the devoted, which may help account for the book's slack quality.

Within the book, the After Life is revealed to resemble nothing so much as a dull Turkey Farm. A character in a Samuel Beckett radio play might have been speaking of *Slapstick's* picture of the Next World when he says: "that's what hell will be like, small chat to the babbling of the Lethe about the good old days when we wished we were dead." Countering this listlessness is Vonnegut's plea for the necessity of all human beings to care for and about one another; a plea for human community, for respect of others, for decency, for order. The great human inventions, according to *Slapstick*, are those which help things to run more smoothly, such as Robert's Rules of Order (SS, pp. 216). Obviously, this is far removed from the Vonnegut of *Breakfast of Champions*, who boasted that he would and had turned "order into chaos."

Slapstick is also a product of the Nixon years—that time when America itself appeared tired and unwilling to face moral issues whether in domestic politics or in foreign policy. President Wilbur Daffodil-11 Swain comments on the only President of the United States ever forced to resign from office:

> . . . Mr. Nixon and his associates had been unbalanced by loneliness of an especially virulent sort. . . . They were not basically criminals . . .. But they yearned to partake of the brotherhood they saw in Organized Crime (SS, p. 166).

Vonnegut will deal more directly and more imaginatively with Watergate, its aftermath, and the issues it raises for Americans and America in *Jailbird*, a more successful novel. The key issue that *Slapstick* joins, however, is the necessity for a viable human community. In several interviews and writings, he tells the story of meeting Sargent Shriver when the latter was the Democratic candidate for Vice President of the United States running against Reagan on the hopelessly doomed McGovern ticket:

> So I told him [Sargent Shriver], and I am afraid he didn't listen, that the number one American killer wasn't cardio-vascular disease, but loneliness. I told him that he and McGovern could swamp the Republicans if they would prom-ise to cure that disease. I even gave him a slogan to put on buttons and bumpers and flags and billboards: Lonesome No More! The rest is history (PS, p. 205).

The grotesque hero of *Slapstick* does take this advice seriously and runs for President of the United States on just such a platform, with just such a slogan—Lonesome No More!—and, as Vonnegut predicted of Shriver and McGovern if they had taken his advice, with just such results: he wins overwhelmingly. As President, Dr. Wilbur Swain goes about the business of creating hundreds of artificial extended families. All those folks who had "never had a friend or relative . . . [who] had to believe all their lives that they were perhaps sent to the wrong Universe, since no one has ever bid them welcome or given them anything to do" (SS, p. 176)—all were now made welcome in their new families with hundreds of siblings and thousands of cousins. Thus did all Americans become "Lonesome No More!"

The United States becomes the site for a series of huge on-going family reunions. For a while, at least, "the intimacies of experience . . . infiltrated . . . the politics of power" instead of the reverse, which is the experience of most people in Vonnegut's America.[7] So while machinery rusts and gravity fluctuates wildly one family of "food-gatherers . . . in and around the ruins of the New York Stock Exchange. . . . fish off docks. They mine for canned goods. They pick fruits and berries . . . They grow their own tomatoes and potatoes and radishes, and little more" (SS, p. 82). And other families find their own best ways to survive in this post-Industrial economy. They also find mutual respect, the importance of which Vonnegut talks about in interviews and in at least one of his public speeches: ". . . love is a rotten substitute for respect," he contends (PS, p. 216).[8]

Vonnegut prefers "respect" because love entails an obligation on the part of the one receiving it to return it. With respect, on the other hand, comes no obligation, but honesty and decency, which are values all can practice. Those who are related in families can be honest, show respect, and demand respect in return. They can also rely upon one another, unlike the former "United States of America, where nobody has a right to rely on anybody else—where everybody learns to make his or her own way" (SS, p. 93).

Besides giving respect to all human beings and the planet, Vonnegut would also have people, at least in *Slapstick* and other novels, turn away from gadgets and machinery and have done with modern technology, which only brings enjoyment for a little while, and focus instead on human relationships. The vision of a world without machines, without modern technology, will be further explored even more imaginatively in *Galápagos*, but in that book human beings will reduce their needs to the basic ones of food, safety, and reproduction. In *Slapstick* human beings, while also reducing their needs to survival ones, have achieved a community in which they value human life, treat one another with respect and decency, and, despite a few madmen who wage wars, manage to live relatively ordered lives.

In *Slapstick* Vonnegut attempts to write serious utopian fiction in which the Earth, thanks to the benign catastrophe of wildly fluctuating gravity, is no longer imperilled by the poison of human technology but is a place where people have learned to live together in extended families and where war is put on a human footing because its human cost is known, acknowledged, and emphasized—rather than remaining an abstraction, as World War II was for many people. In *Slapstick* people who volunteer for war, who want to kill, are rejected as unfit for combat, and only those who recognize the terrible price in human life that wars exact are allowed to fight. With extended families of thousands of relatives spread all across the country, each family will have relatives on any side of any war and hence must realize that if they fight they will injure and kill human beings related to them, rather than the less-than-human enemy created by the propaganda on both sides of World War II. It is "a game our dreams remade" (SS, p. 230).

Besides humanizing war, such extended families also allow the pure in heart to survive various ordeals. Thus Melody, the King of Candlesticks' granddaughter, makes the incredible journey from Michigan to New York on foot encountering as she goes "relatives everywhere":

> They would feed her and point the way.
> One would give her a raincoat. another . . . a sweater and a magnetic compass. . . .
> Another would give her a needle and thread, and a gold thimble, too.
> Another would row her across the Harlem River to the Island of Death, at the risk of his own life (SS, p. 243).

All the elements from folk tales of Good winning out over Evil because of remaining innocent are here. As is the final vision of the hero himself celebrating his one-hundreth birthday with a thousand lit candles, "Standing among all those tiny, wavering lights, I felt as though I were God, up to my knees in the Milky Way" (SS, p. 228). The novel is very much a fairy-tale story of a blighted land placed under a curse by a wicked witch until rescued by an innocent hero who, after reforming the society, dies leaving a scrap of verse behind:

"And how did we then face the odds,
"Of man's rude slapstick, yes, and God's?
"Quite at home and unafraid,
"Thank you,
"In a game our dreams remade" (SS, p. 230).

Slapstick is, thus, Vonnegut's vision of a better world through fantasy, and as such, this fiction gives what Robert Scholes calls "feedback," which he defines as "a means toward correcting our behavior in the world."[9] The "feedback" of this particular novel, however, could become clearer for most readers if the "game" or the "dream" were not blurred because of the ill-defined way it is told. Unlike *Slaughterhouse-Five*, where Vonnegut puts himself clearly in the role of narrator with a minor part in the action or in *Breakfast of Champions* where he is narrator and plays a major role in the action, in *Slapstick* he apparently writes the Prologue, daydreams the story, then finishes it in the Epilogue. His is a formal, conventional relation of author to narrator to story rather than that of a prominent "character in [his] . . . works," which he talked about when he announced his return to fiction writing (TT, p. xv). Also contributing to the "blurring" is his earlier dismissal of Kilgore Trout in *Breakfast of Champions*, for the devices of the shrinking microscopic Chinese and the Martian invasion in the form of flu germs (SS, p. 234) would each make a far better plot for a failed Kilgore Trout novel than they do as part of a serious book by Kurt Vonnegut.[10] Finally, as mentioned before, *Slapstick* appears a gentle, quiet, but occasionally tired book. While Vonnegut does not again return to the frenetic activity of *Breakfast of Champions* or *The Sirens of Titan*, he will go on to write with far more authority in *Jailbird* and *Deadeye Dick*, with more consistency in a well-developed fantasy in *Galápagos*, and with more unity and craft in *Bluebeard*.

Slapstick remains, however, an important book in the Vonnegut canon because of its focus on the central issue of the loneliness of Americans, which Vonnegut so often mentions. "No matter how old we

71

are, we are going to be bored and lonely during what remains of our lives" (PS, p. 180), he contends, and as a result, Americans have a deep-seated need for a real human community that genuinely cares about people (PS, pp. 180-82, 204-7, 215-16). Still, *Slapstick* will probably continue to be, like *Happy Birthday, Wanda June*, more interesting as a transitional than as a successful work. Time has simply proven his assertion untrue that "this [novel] is the closest I will ever come to writing an autobiography" (SS, p. 7). *Palm Sunday*, published some years after *Slapstick*, is a splendid, revealing autobiography in which Vonnegut talks about himself as writer, father, husband, and human being. He also grades his work and in so doing gives both *Slapstick* and *Happy Birthday, Wanda June* a "D," *Breakfast of Champions* a "C," while *Between Time and Timbuktu* goes entirely unmentioned (probably because Vonnegut only contributed to the script rather than writing the whole program), (PS, p. 312)—judgments that many readers would say are far too harsh. Richard Giannone, for example, one of the most perceptive critics of Vonnegut's work, sees *Breakfast of Champions* and *Slapstick* as providing "a fictive guide to our lost culture" (*Vonnegut*, p. 126)—a large claim which he substantiates by a close reading of these novels.[11] Other critics and readers have also defended other works, especially *Breakfast of Champions*, finding in them genuine delight and significance.

NOTES

1 Clive Barnes, "Stage: 'Happy Birthday, Wanda June,'" *The New York Times*, 9 Oct. 1970, p. 43.

2 Quoted in Mel Gussow, "Vonnegut is Having Fun Doing a Play," *The New York Times*, 6 October 1970, p. 65.

3 Charlie Reilly, "Two Conversations with Kurt Vonnegut," *College Literature*, 7.1 (Winter 1980), p. 15.

4 "Writer's Workshop," SCTV-PBS, 1980.

5 Jerome Klinkowitz, "Vonnegut in America," in *Vonnegut in America*, ed. Jerome Klinkowitz and Donald L. Lawler (New York: Delacorte, 1977) p. 25.

6 "Vonnegut's *Breakfast of Champions*: The Conversion of Heliogabalus," *Critique*, 18.3 (1979), 108.

7 Richard Giannone, *Vonnegut: A Preface to His Novels* (Port Washington: Kennikat Press, 1977), p. 124.

8 Compare SS, pp. 74-75.

9 *Fabulation and Metafiction* (Urbana: University of Illinois Press, 1979), p. 214.

10 In an interview published in 1973, Vonnegut talks about writing a Kilgore Trout novel with a plot similar to *Slapstick's* (WF&G), pp. 247-249.

11 op. cit., pp. 98-126.

VI. "An Air of Defeat"
Jailbird and *Deadeye Dick*

Commenting on his mother's suicide and his father's withdrawal from actively participating in life after the Great Depression wiped out his career as an architect, Vonnegut concludes: "So an air of defeat has always been a companion of mine" (JB, p. 13).[1] Although all his novels share this "air of defeat," nowhere is it more apparent than in *Deadeye Dick* whose hero, Rudy Waltz, effectively stops living at age twelve when he commits a double murder, and in *Jailbird* whose hero, Walter Starbuck, lives life in a minor key, experiences almost everything at secondhand, and never gets very deeply involved in life or with other people. As a recidivist, Starbuck leaves jail only to return to jail. Moreover, he has a completely undistinguished, inconsequential career, a so-so marriage, an impossible son. He knows defeat continually, especially when out of work for many years; experiences success only briefly as vice-president of the Down Home Records division of RAMJAC (the world's largest corporation); and hesitates to draw many lessons from experience except to believe: "We are here for no purpose, unless we can invent one" (JB, p. 278). In contrast to *Cat's Cradle*, which concludes with a "Bang!" signalling the end of the world, *Deadeye Dick* ends with a mild protest against human stupidity and irresponsibility, while *Jailbird* concludes with a barely heard, if heartfelt, "whimper," for the life of Walter F. Starbuck sounds a note much like that of the prothonotary warblers that appear in the novel: their "song . . . is notoriously monotonous . . . . Still—they are capable of expressing heartbreak—within strict limits, of course" (JB, p. 197).

Yet, Starbuck does inspire the love and affectionate loyalty of three women: besides his wife, Ruth, there are also his early love, Sarah Wyatt, and his first serious girlfriend, Mary Kathleen. It is Mary Kathleen who, with her dying words, accurately assesses him: "You couldn't help it that you were born without a heart. At least you tried to believe what the people with hearts believed—so you were a good man just the same" (JB, p. 261).[2] And with all his air of defeat and his life lived in a minor key, Starbuck remains capable of genuine emotion. For example, when he hugs Mary Kathleen on the streets of New York and finds himself "embracing a bundle of dry twigs that was wrapped in rags" (JB, p. 182), his reaction is warmly human as he recognizes the fragility of all human beings and of all love: "I was crying for the first time since I had found my wife dead in bed one morning . . ." (JB, p. 182). He is also capable of quiet indignation at the way humans willfully ignore serious, real problems: "You know what is going to finally going to kill this planet? . . . A total lack of seriousness . . . Nobody gives a damn anymore about what's really going on, what's going to happen next, or how we ever got into such a mess in the first place" (JB, p. 280).

Like most of Vonnegut's novels, *Jailbird* takes place in the near future and makes excellent use of the fantastic in developing character and plot. Kilgore Trout in his newest identity as "Bob Fender," lifer, reappears despite his banishment at the end of *Breakfast of Champions*. In every novel in which he appears, Trout has a different address—Cape Cod, Massachusetts; Illium, New York; Georgia; Ohio—, a different job—newspaper distributor, worker in a greenstamp redemption center, Nobel prize winner in medicine, and convict—, a different age—forties, fifties, thirties—, different physical appearance, different personality, and even a different name. The only consistency he enjoys is as a science-fiction writer. In *Jailbird* Fender-Trout's stories comment in humorous ways on the serious issues of adult irresponsibility for the life on this planet and the deification of wealth.

In one of Trout's stories, the inhabitants of the planet Vicuna show off their wealth by burning time, exactly as people on Earth demonstrate their wealth by depleting natural resources, driving species to extinction, and mortgaging the future to play frivolously today. The Vicunan judge's lament about his race applies equally well to Earthlings: "we lived as though there were no tomorrow" (JB, p. 99). Parallel to the acknowledgement of such irresponsible action lies the knowledge of the difficult, perhaps impossible, task of changing a society whose consumers worship wealth above all other values, including scientific discoveries and original thought. Trout's story, "Asleep at the Switch," satirizes these negative values: Albert Einstein dies and goes to heaven where he meets a pompous heavenly accountant who tells him how he wasted his time by not investing his money wisely:

75

he could have become a billionaire, if only he had gotten a second mortgage on his house in Bern, Switzerland, in Nineteen-hundred and Five, and invested the money in known uranium deposits before telling the world that E=MC².

"But there you were—asleep at the switch again," said the auditor (JB, pp. 225-226).

If Trout's story satirizes the worship of wealth, then, the fantastic Mary Kathleen O'Looney illustrates the glaring disparity in the United States between enormous wealth, which she "enjoys" as Mrs. Jack Graham, and abysmal poverty, which she also experiences as Mary Kathleen O'Looney.[3] She is, however, unable to live a happy, carefree, normal life as either person. In fact, she becomes a shopping bag lady as a way of keeping alive by hiding from all those who would gladly kill her: "On this particular planet, where money mattered more than anything, the nicest person imaginable might suddenly get the idea of wringing her neck so that their loved ones might live in comfort" (JB, p. 193).

As a shopping bag lady, Mary Kathleen O'Looney is a fantastic character who represents a clear "departure from consensus reality" about such people.[4] Such women do not own most of the world's largest corporation nor can they when about to die, ". . . pick the exact time" of death, once the process of dying has begun (JB, p. 260.) She also proves a fine vehicle for Vonnegut's satire on both the out-of-control quality of the American corporate world and the ineffectiveness of the innocent revolutionary.[5] As the majority stockholder in the world's largest corporation, her one instruction to her officer in charge is "Acquire! Acquire! Acquire!" which he does with amazing, positive results. Like a fairy-godmother with a magic wand, she creates instant-Vice Presidents of RAMJAC with no more qualification than whatever their immediate situation might be. Thus a nightclerk in a run-down hotel, who has been on the job a mere three weeks, becomes Vice President of the Hilton Department of the Hospitality Associates, Ltd., Division of RAMJAC, and a salesman for matchbook cover advertising becomes vice-president of the Diamond Match Division of RAMJAC. In the two years that Starbuck works as vice-president of Down Home Records Division of RAMJAC, which includes *The New York Times*, Universal Pictures, Ringling Bros. and Barnum and

Bailey circus, Dell Publishing, and a catfood company, although he has no relevant experience whatsoever, he manages to bring in a twenty-three percent return on capital investment along with two Nobel prizes in literature, "eleven platinum records, forty-two gold records, twenty-two Oscars, eleven National Book Awards, two American League pennants, two National League pennants, two World Series, and fifty-three Grammies!" (JB, pp. 247-248, 268). "Think of that," as the narrator might say. Yet such happenings are really no more fantastic than the bizarre world of high finance with its acquisitions, mergers, and leveraged buyouts as reported on television, in the news magazines or in the daily papers.[6]

Jailbird is also a novel about the forgotten "little people" who try to survive in difficult times without either a "golden parachute" or the now-famous "safety-net" of welfare programs. Mary Kathleen O'Looney's homelessness somewhat reflects the callousness with which the Nixon administration viewed the poor. It was Nixon who "taught us to resent the poor for not solving their own problems," says Vonnegut (WF&G, p. 272). Like those "useless" men, those victims of the Great Depression, who in the 1930s wandered the country first in search of work and then later simply to survive, these currently "useless" members of American society in the 1970s and 1980s attempt to live on their own on the streets.

For those who have no homes, no families, no fortunes, becoming a shopping bag lady represents the dead end of a hard life. Richard Schechner quotes from a description in a Sunday *New York Times* of "the nightly rituals of some homeless 'bag ladies'" in a New York public lavatory:

At 11 p.m. the attendant goes off duty and women rise from separate niches and head for the bathroom. There they disrobe and wash their clothes and bodies. Depending on the length of the line at the hand dryers, they wait to dry their clothes, put them in their bags or wear them wet. One woman cleans and wraps her ulcerated legs with paper towels every night.

The most assertive claim toilet cubicles, line them with newspapers for privacy and warmth and sleep curled around the basin. Once they are taken, the rest sleep along the walls, one on a box directly beneath the hand dryer which she pushed for warm air. One of the women regularly cleans the floors, sinks and toilets so that no traces of their uncustomary use remain.[7]

Vonnegut looks at these unfortunate people and criticizes the economic system that allows such terrible deprivation and misfortune to exist in one of the wealthiest countries in the world:

Ragged regiments of them [shopping bag ladies] had been produced accidentally, and to no imaginable purpose, by the great engine of the economy. Another part of the machine was spitting out unrepentent murderers ten years old, and dope fiends and child batterers and many other bad things. People claimed to be investigating. Unspecified repairs were to be made at some future time (JB, p. 182).[8]

Besides illustrating the failure of the free-market economy to take care of the disadvantaged poor in her person as a nameless shopping bag lady, O'Looney also, as Mrs. Jack Graham, illustrates the failure of the naive revolutionary to change this pernicious system. All her life she remained true to her ideal, working towards the revolution every day (JB, p. 184), yet her method, calling people she meets on the street "capitalist fats," does not appear to change much if anything—most people cannot even understand what she is saying! At death, through her will, she hopes to alter radically the economic fortunes of the United States' citizens by leaving "The RAMJAC Corporation to its rightful owners, the American people" (JB, p. 260), but such an idealistic plan is clearly doomed to fail, for, as in *God Bless You, Mr. Rosewater*, money proves an impotent force for good: "Most of those businesses, rigged only to make profits, were as indifferent to the needs of the people as, say, thunderstorms. Mary Kathleen might as well have left one-fifth of the weather to the people," says Starbuck. He continues:

The businesses of RAMJAC, by their very nature, were as unaffected by the joys and tragedies of human beings as the rain that fell on the night that Madeiros and Sacco and Vanzetti died in an electric chair. It would have rained anyway.

The economy is a thoughtless weather system—and nothing more.

Some joke on the people, to give them such a thing" (JB, p. 272).

Neither Mary Kathleen with her unreflective gift of the RAMJAC Corporation to "the American people" as if they were a first cousin or a daughter nor Starbuck with his naive joining of the Communist party in his youth succeed in changing the way society operates economically or socially. O'Looney's naivity may be understandable and her generosity commendible. Nevertheless, she fails totally to achieve her desired results. Rather than helping the poor as she intended, she benefits only those, the "capitalist fats," whom she held most in contempt all her life, as the vast bulk of her legacy goes to hire twenty-thousand new bureaucrats, most of them already rich lawyers. Those poor unfortunates such as herself, the shopping bag ladies and homeless old men, will never see one dime of her fortune.

Jailbird thus offers a clear warning against allowing the idealism of youth to become a guide for action in maturity: O'Looney lives up to her name and fails to change the world with her fortune; "Bob Fender," the veterinarian and science–fiction writer (Kilgore Trout) lands in jail for life because of naively sheltering a North Korean spy, as if she were a wounded doe (JB, pp. 102-104). Walter F. Starbuck sends his friend to jail by naively naming him as a known communist before Nixon's Congressional Investigating Committee. Later, he proves equally naive in accepting a position in the Nixon administration as a "reward" for his part in helping to bring an obscure freshman Congressman onto the front pages of the nation's newspapers and from there ultimately to be elected President of the United States.

Moreover, Starbuck learns the wrong lesson from his experience since he will later go to jail himself rather than expose some of the Watergate conspirators—this is indeed "a book . . . for tears!" (JB, p. 188). And while *Mother Night* is a study and, by inference, a warning against the schizophrenic personality, *Jailbird* is a study in naivity and idealism and a warning against each as an inappropriate guide for adult behavior.[9] "I believed," says the youthful Starbuck, "that there could be no higher calling in a democracy than to a lifetime in government" (JB, p. 47)—a truly idealistic statement of the concept of "government service." While this ideal is one worth following, it is also necessary to watch out for the Richard Nixons of this world who, when they come to power, may take advantage of such "ideals" to further their own nefarious ends, thereby completely subverting the ideal.

Richard Milhous Nixon, an American isolato, as solitary as Melville's Bartleby, was the "first President," according to Vonnegut, "to hate the American people" (WF&G, p. xxiii). A notoriously humorless man, except perhaps in his daughter's eyes (JB, p. 242), Vonnegut credits him with "one good joke" that, of course, he writes for him.[10] In an emergency meeting called to discuss how to handle the Ohio National Guard's killing of four Kent State University students, Starbuck, as the president's youth adviser,[11] became so nervous that he

> soon had three cigarettes going all at once, and was in the process of lighting a fourth.
>
> The President himself at last noticed the column of smoke rising from my place, and stopped all business to stare at me. . . .
>
> "We will pause in our business," he said, "while our special advisor on youth affairs gives us a demonstration of how to put out a campfire."
>
> There was laughter all around (JB, p. 76).

Throughout *Jailbird*, Vonnegut illustrates some of the corrosive effects of the Nixon presidency within the larger contexts of the McCarthy-Nixon witchhunts of the fifties and the Sacco and Vanzetti executions of the twenties. The lessons of history appear no more comforting here than those that led Bokonon to exclaim in *Cat's Cradle*: "History. . . . Read it and weep!" (CC, p. 168). For Kilgore Trout—no matter what his age, job or personality—never wrote as fantastic a story of the miscarriage of justice as the actual historical account of the trial and deaths of Sacco and Vanzetti who were innocent of the charges of murder, yet sentenced to die; whose judge had already determined their guilt, before the trial began and later bragged after sentencing them to death: "Did you see what I did to those anarchist bastards the other day?" (JB, p. 222).

The execution of Sacco and Vanzetti did not "cause an irresistible mania for justice to the common people" (JB, p. 51), but rather became lost in the dusty pages of history— much as the Dresden massacre was "lost" until Vonnegut published *Slaughterhouse-Five*, thus helping bring it into the light of day. Nor did the forced resignation of Nixon's Vice-President Spiro Agnew, the various Watergate convictions, nor even Nixon's own impending impeachment and subsequent resigning in disgrace do much, if anything, to usher in a new era of honesty or sensitivity to the public trust among political appointees, as shown in the corruption, inditements, and resignations of the scandal-ridden Reagan administration. As Vonnegut says elsewhere, "vanity rather than wisdom determines how the world is run" (PS, p. 299).

In such a world, where "the best lack all conviction and the worst are full of passionate intensity," where the drive for riches and power appears to supersede all other values, perhaps the most anyone can hope for is that "courtesy will prevail," which, Vonnegut tells us, is the theme of all his novels: "Love may fail, but courtesy will prevail" (JB, p. 10).[12] Within *Jailbird*, itself, one of the few times when courtesy does prevail and the profit motive does not operate and no one tries to grab power occurs not in the government nor in a corporation, but in a New York City coffee shop that Starbuck visits during his first day out of jail. Here courtesy reigns supreme: "I had the feeling that if Frankenstein's monster crashed into the coffee shop through a brick wall, all anybody would say to him was, 'You sit down here, Lambchop, and I'll bring you your coffee right away'" (JB, p. 166). Such small courtesies, such little pleasures, Vonnegut suggests, "can have the most profound effects,"[13] for they help to keep life going even when that life, like Walter F. Starbuck's "expresses heartbreak" if only in a minor key.

Such courtesy is noticably absent from the world of *Deadeye Dick* except in the hero, Rudy Waltz. The novel proves to be a quiet lament for his unlived life, a life in which nothing gives satisfaction and everything that looks as if it might be good turns out to be "booby trapped" (DD, p. 133):

> I concluded that the best thing for me and for those around me was to want nothing, to be enthusiastic about nothing, to be as unmotivated as possible, in fact, so that I would never again hurt anyone.

To put it another way: I wasn't to touch anything on this planet, man, woman, child, artifact, animal, vegetable, or mineral—since it was very likely to be connected to a push-pull detonator and an explosive charge" (DD, p 112).

"Within strict limits," Rudy's life echoes faintly the lament of Job as he experienced the loss of his children, fortune, position in society, faith, and all he held dear:

> Why did I not die at birth,
>   come forth from the womb and expire?
> . . . .
> For then I should have lain down and been quiet;
>   I should have slept; then I should have been at rest,
> with kings and counselors of the earth
>   who rebuilt ruins for themselves (Job 3.11-14; RSV trans.).

Rudy's life is over the minute he fires the rifle at twelve years old that kills the pregnant housewife on Mother's Day. Never again will he do anything on his own. He becomes, as he says, a "neuter"—never knowing love, never having any fun, never tasting any of the sins or delights of life (DD, p. 99). His story as a neuter ends, he decides, either at Celia Hoover's funeral, when he experiences foregiveness, or with the death of his mother; all the rest is epilogue (DD, p. 210).[14]

The great crises in his life, those painful moments of confrontation with others, he presents as playlets (DD, p. 83), a technique that creates distance between those difficult-to-recall events and the person to whom they happened. In his first brief play, the police, after smearing his face with ink while fingerprinting him, throw him in a cage in the basement of the police station, and then invite good or important citizens to come down and taunt him to help make him realize that he is "a defective human being" (DD, p. 79). The ultimate confrontation occurs when the bereaved husband of the woman he accidentally killed arrives. The second crisis happens in the New York City apartment of his brother, Felix, on the afternoon of the premiere of his play, "Katmandu," when he overhears a conversation about himself—one which points out his failings. The third confrontation occurs between Celia Hoover barefoot, suffering from withdrawal symptoms, asking him as the all-night drugstore clerk for drugs (when he refuses, she wrecks the place). The fourth and last confrontation takes place at her funeral, as Felix, high on drugs, breaks down. The fact that two out of four of these painful incidents involve drugs emphasizes the crucial role that "pharmaceutical buffoonery" plays in the novel (DD, p. 191).

In times of crisis, Rudy thus adopts this fiction that he is merely an actor speaking lines in a sequence of events written and directed by someone else.[15] But, as Bokonon remarked in *Cat's Cradle*: "God never wrote a good play in His Life" (CC, p. 161), and the parts Rudy is given all involve his personal and, usually, deep humiliation.[15]

Rudy's excruciatingly isolated life recalls that of the hero of the most famous story of isolation in American literature, "Bartleby, the Scivener" by Herman Melville.[16] Bartleby may once have worked as a Subordinate Clerk in the Dead Letter Office of the United States' Post Office in Washington, D.C. Can anything be more depressing, asks the narrator, than the "continual handling [of] these dead letters, and assorting them for the flames? ... On errands of life, these letters speed to death," exactly as Bartleby himself sped to death as more and more he "prefers not to" participate in work, leisure or life itself—as Rudy "prefers not to" participate in life.[17]

Instead, life appears to wall both Rudy and Bartleby in—the latter literally and figuratively, until he dies of physical, emotional and spiritual starvation curled up in a foetal position facing the base of a brick wall "of amazing thickness ... his head touching the cold stones." If, instead of starving, Rudy grows fat on his own cooking, his motivation remains similar to Bartleby's, for he has no emotional life and believes, like Bartleby and Job, that he does not "really belong on this particular planet" (DD, p. 176).

Rudy's life, so empty of love and most of the things associated with it—such as intimate relationships of all kinds, close friendship, a sense of vocation, and a commitment to living—has a vast hole, an emptiness at its very center that he attempts to fill not only with cooking, but also with scat singing. The scat singing—nonsense syllables to chase the blues—helps fill time; exactly as cooking to feed others, especially his parents, helps fill the gaps in his story where love or life should be. The recipes, which he includes as part of his life story, are part of his witty commentary on life and the way others value him. They act "as musical interludes for the salivary glands"—

a culinary pause in the narrative (DD, p. ix). They also serve to break any possible emotional involvement by author or reader in the story. The message of these devices is clear: Rudy is NOT involved in life at any level.

One of the best epigraphs for Rudy's life is an extraordinary poem by Chidiock Tichborne written—tradition has it—in the Tower of London the night before he was executed. In it he laments his lost life, for his, like Rudy's, appears over before he had an opportunity to live it:

My prime of youth is but a frost of cares,
  My feast of joy is but a dish of pain,
My crop of corn is but a field of tares,
  And all my good is but vain hope of gain;
     The day is past, and yet I saw no sun,
     And now I live, and now my life is done.

My tale was heard and yet it was not told,
  My fruit is fallen and yet my leaves are green,
My youth is spent and yet I am not old,
  I saw the world and yet I was not seen;
     My thread is cut and yet it is not spun,
     And now I live, and now my life is done.[18]

Parallel to Rudy's failure to live life to the full, or even at all, is the country's failure to take account of the conditions necessary for life and to nurture them. Instead, the United States appears hellbent on inventing better and better engines of destruction, such as the atom and neutron bombs, and on placing lethal weapons in the hands of irresponsible people. Rudy's sardonic removed vision may be the only possible one on a planet that displays so proudly the "complete lack of seriousness" of which Walter F. Starbuck speaks in *Jailbird*, where adults, such as Otto Waltz, encourage and extoll the virtues of madmen, such as Hitler, and their murderous hate-filled schemes, where parents give their children loaded rifles to play with as toys, where people seriously advocate selling armor-piercing bullets, plastic guns and Saturday Night Specials to any and all,[19] and where governments test tanks on good farmland and bombs on civilian cities.

At the beginning of the novel, two juxtaposed incidents suggest its theme of the disastrous effects of wishful thinking as a substitute for human responsibility: Mrs. Eleanor Roosevelt comes to lunch at the Waltz household on Mother's Day, 1944. At the dinner table, she shares her belief in progress and the prospects for a better world after the war (DD, p. 59), while Otto Waltz "said most of the things the National Rifle Association still says about how natural and beautiful it is for Americans to have love affairs with guns" (DD, p. 60). At the very moment of their talking, Rudy, an inexperienced twelve year old, sits with a loaded rifle in the cupola at the top of the house believing equally foolishly that "If I aimed at nothing, then nothing is what I would hit" (DD, p. 64).

Time reveals that all these beliefs—in progress, in the beauty of America's love affair with guns, and in the impossibility of hitting anything unless one aimed at it—were equally without foundation. Rudy's aimless bullet kills not one but two; guns have been used to commit numerous crimes and assassinations, including public figures and presidents; the world after World War Two was not a better place in which to live.[20] The John Fortune farm in Midland City becomes symbolic of the kind of "progress" enjoyed in the United States from the thirties through the seventies: in the thirties the farm is self-sustaining and productive until the Great Depression wipes it out and Fortune sets off in search of Shangri-La. In the forties it becomes a tank proving ground in the service of the United States armed forces fighting in World War Two. In the sixties it becomes "Avondale," archetypal suburban tract housing, made up of "little shitboxes," as Rudy describes them. Then in the eighties it becomes part of the test area for the neutron bomb that may have been dropped by the United States goverment because Midland City was the least objectionable place on which to test it (DD, p. 234).[21]

Vonnegut satirizes the mentality that insists on testing bigger and bigger weapons, on trying things out when there is no way of determining the long or sometimes even the short-term consequences.[22] "We are," as Rudy concludes at the end of his story, "still living in the Dark Ages . . . they haven't ended yet" (DD, p. 240). Individually and together, like the ghost of Will Fairchild killed while doing an airplane stunt, people search in vain for a parachute, but there is none. In such a world it becomes, as Rudy Waltz observes, "too easy, when alive, to make perfecty horrible mistakes" (DD, p. 6). So the government and a twelve-year-old boy both have much in common with this old nursery rhyme about acting without taking responsibility for the results:

> I shot an arrow
>   in the air.
> It fell to earth
>   I know not where.

But such acts have far-reaching consequences. To win the war, the United States developed and used the atomic bomb with on-going consequences beyond anyone's imagining.[23] In the Avondale shitbox where Rudy and his mother live, a fancy, highly radioactive mantlepiece eventually causes a braintumor in his mother leading to her highly erratic behavior.

> With a lot of luck, and the help of a few honest people, we were able to trace the cement that went into the mantlepiece all the way back to Oak Ridge, Tennessee, where pure uranium 235 was produced for the bomb they dropped on Hiroshima in 1945. The government somehow allowed the cement to be sold off as war surplus, even though many people had known how hot it was.
>
> In this case, the government was about as careless as a half-wit boy up in a cupola with a loaded Springfield rifle— on Mother's Day (DD, pp. 214-215).

Not surprisingly, "an air of defeat" dominates both novels, for we are indeed "still in the Dark Ages," as Vonnegut maintains (DD, p. 240), as long as humans and governments continue to act irresponsibly, as in *Deadeye Dick*, or refuse to take themselves and their responsibility for life on this planet seriously, as in *Jailbird*.

NOTES

1 Katherine Hume contends that "because of its timing, his [Vonnegut's] mother's suicide appears to have been a gesture directed at her son." "Kurt Vonnegut and the Myths and Symbols of Meaning," *Texas Studies in Literature and Language*, 24.4 (Winter 1982), p. 433.

2 Perhaps Walter Starbuck is a positive illustration of the moral Vonnegut gave for *Mother Night*: "We are what we pretend to be" (MN, p. v).

3 The two sides of Mary Kathleen O'Looney illustrate Paul Fussell's thesis that both the uppermost and the lowermost economic and social classes in the United States are invisible. See Paul Fussell, *Class* (New York: Summit Books, 1983).

4 From Katherine Hume's "working definition" of fantasy: *"Fantasy is any departure from consensus reality."* *Mimesis and Fantasy* (New York: Methuen, 1984), p. 21.

5 For another satiric view of the inexplicable world (in human terms) of high finance, compare Malichi Constant and his father's "luck" for making money in *The Sirens of Titan*.

6 See, for example, almost any edition of a weekly news magazine in December, 1988, for stories of the "Greatest Buyout" of the century, e.g., *Newsweek*, December, 1988. No wonder Sarah Wyatt said to Starbuck in great perplexity: "Money is so strange. . . . Does it make any sense to you?" (JB, p. 106.)

7 *The End of Humanism* (New York: Performing Arts Journal Publications, 1982), p. 114.

8 This out-of-control economy has remained a continuing preoccupation of Vonnegut's from *Player Piano*, and *God Bless You, Mr. Rosewater* to this novel.

9 For a vivid exception to this failure to meld experience and idealism see the meeting between Vonnegut and Powers Hapgood (JB, pp. 10-19). See also p. 54 for a further discussion of Hapgood in relation to *God Bless You, Mr. Rosewater*.

10 In an essay on the comedy team, Bob and Ray, Vonnegut reveals that he once applied for a job as a writer on their show; he does not say if he ever applied for a job as a writer for Mr. Nixon (PS, p. 141).

11 Vonnegut's model for Nixon's "special advisor," whom Nixon never consults, may have been Secretary of the Interior Wally Hickel who in a "well-publicized letter . . . sent to Nixon, the President, . . . recommended [that President Nixon] ought to make himself more accessible to youth and to members of his Cabinet, while Agnew's abrasive alliteration should be heard less." Aside from the publicity, the letter produced no descernible results. Summarized in William E. Leuchtenburg, *A Troubled Feast: American Society Since 1945* (Boston: Little, Brown, 1983), p. 247.

12 This evaluation was contained in a letter sent to Vonnegut by "a young stranger named John Figler, of Crown Point, Indiana" (JB, pp. 9-10).

13 Jerome Klinkowitz, *Kurt Vonnegut* (New York: Methuen, 1982), p. 81.

14 For a quite different though unsubstantiated reading of Rudy's life, see Lawrence R. Broer, *Sanity Plea: Schizophrenia in the Novels of Kurt Vonnegut* (Ann Arbor: UMI Research Press, 1989), pp. 137-150, but especially 141-142.

15 Broer's view of the plays is that "art has allowed Rudy to absorb and transform trauma into healing, personal truth . . .." Ibid., p. 146.

16 Melville uses the phrase from Job: "with kings and councillors" to suggest the desperate plight of Bartleby. It applies equally well to Rudy Waltz. All quotations from and references to Melville's short story may be found in the *Concise Anthology of American Literature*, ed. George McMichael, 2nd ed. (New York: Macmillan, 1985), pp. 590-614.

17 For example, he reveals: "I have never made love to anyone. Nor have I tasted alcohol . . ." (DD, p. 99); and, later, "it seemed safest and wisest to be as cold as ice . . . to everyone" (DD, p. 110).

18 *Elizabethan Lyrics: a Critical Anthology*, ed. Kenneth Muir (London: George G. Harrap, 1952), p. 175.

19 These positions are seriously maintained and defended by the National Rifle Association; see, for example, *Washington Report*, 14.2 (Summer 1988) published by Handgun Control, Inc., Washington, D.C., for accounts of NRA opposition to banning armor-piercing, "cop-killer" bullets, p. 6; NRA opposition to banning plastic handguns, p. 3; and NRA opposition to a waiting period before approving handgun sales, p. 1.

20 Despite all the National Rifle Association propaganda about the neutrality of guns, it is impossible to imagine Rudy killing anyone had he not had a loaded rifle in his hands.

21 Reflecting on the effects of the neutron bomb which killed the population, but left the property and buildings of Midland City intact, Rudy asks: "Does it matter to anyone or anything that all those [lives were lost] . . . so suddenly? Since all the property is undamaged, has the world lost anything it loved?" (DD, p. 34). His question echoes Mona's at the end of *Cat's Cradle* as "she went strolling up among the petrified [because killed by ice-nine] thousands . . .. She paused . . . and called . . . 'Would you wish any of these alive again, if you could? Answer me quickly. Not quick enough with your answer,' she called playfully, . . . and, still laughing a little, she touched her finger to the ground, straightened up, and touched her finger to her lips and died" (CC, p. 183).

22 It appears scarcely believable today, but in the fifties people were invited to watch atomic tests in the Nevada desert and other places! Later the government wanted such testing kept secret, because of the unforeseen consequences to human, plant and animal life. As Vonnegut remarked about the destruction of Dresden: "A secret from whom?"

23 For a carefully considered defense of the use of the atom bomb to shorten the war, see Brian Aldiss, *Forgotten Life* (London: Gollancz, 1988), pp. 178-181.

VII. Joy and Acceptance
Galápagos and *Bluebeard*

Galápagos is a book for joy—an exuberant comic look at the dubious future of mankind. Returning to science-fiction, after several fantastic novels, Vonnegut brings to it a sense of play without the earlier freneticism of *The Sirens of Titan* or the cataclysmic destruction of *Cat's Cradle* or the predictability of *Player Piano*. Gone also is the Talfamadorean or God's eye view of all time found in *Slaughterhouse-Five* and in its place is a sweeping view back to the near future from one-million years ahead.

In fiction, the future is always a metaphor.[1] Vonnegut uses this metaphor to suggest the unpredictability, especially from a human prespective, of things to come and the necessity for all creatures to live in a right relationship to the planet: in other words, adapt or die—the fittest survive. In the future of *Galápagos,* humans turn into less destructive, far more lovable, furry, polymorphosely perverse, aquatic creatures, thus ensuring their own survival, that of other beings, and of the very planet itself. Vonnegut clearly uses the far future to tell readers about the present, a present in which humans appear anything but "lovable." His book is, thus, a timely warning against human beings destroying what there is left to destroy, which ultimately is life itself.[2]

Unlike many novels that contain a similar warning, *Galápagos* does not, however, postulate an idealized picture of humankind reverting to some preindustrial age where most good things remain, but society becomes feudal in outlook, organization, and technology. (*Slapstick*, his weakest novel, comes closest to such a picture of a simple, non-machine civilization.) In *Galápagos* Vonnegut starts from the now-familiar premise that unless humans stop destroying their habitant, polluting it with their own garbage, and increasing its temperature, then, this beautiful, fragile planet will become uninhabitable—a theme familiar from *Cat's Cradle, Breakfast of Champions, Slapstick,* and *Jailbird*.[3] Rather than allow this tragic series of events to run its course, evolution itself, in Vonnegut's novel, steps in to ensure that only the fittest survive—which does not include those big brained human beings! As the narrator says, "this was a very innocent planet, except for those great big brains" (GG, p. 9).

The disaster that precipitates the change in evolution appears, on balance, benign, unlike in *Deadeye Dick* where a neutron bomb wipes out Midland City within an uncaring, callous, indifferent world or in *Cat's Cradle* where human greed and stupidity lead to death by freezing of all life on the planet or in *Slaughterhouse-Five* where the universe ends when a Tralfamadorean accidentally blows it up. In *Galápagos* the human population on most of the planet is unable to reproduce, hence dies out, but a small remnant does survive on the new ark of the Galápagos Islands where it evolves into the new smaller brained, aquatic creatures who have neither hands nor fingers with which to damage the environment. As fast swimmers, humans live in harmony with the natural world, returned to their first and most natural element, the Earth's seas. The fittest survive, as Darwin predicted they would.

Leon Trout, son of Kilgore Trout, narrates *Galápagos* as "a ghost in the rigging" of a ghost ship sailing the seas. When he writes about the "Voyage of the Century," he does so without paper, pen, typewriter, or computer but with his index finger in the air. He is certainly the ideal omniscient, invisible narrator able to read minds, descern motivation, predict events accurately, and have the widest possible frame for his tale: "a million years in the future." He describes himself as "Nature's experiment with voyerism, as my father was Nature's experiment with ill-founded self-confidence" (GG, p. 82). As he writes on air, he has not "the slightest hint that there might actually be a reader somewhere. There isn't one. There can't be one" (GG, p. 257).

Trout's writing on air for no possible audience parallels the story of the greatest artist in the world who could draw only in water. Tom Wolfe gives his satiric version of the tale in *The Painted Word*:

> Suppose the greatest artist in the history of the world, impoverished and unknown at the time, had been sitting at a table in the old Automat at Union Square [in New York City], cadging some free water and hoping to cop a leftover crust of toasted corn muffin . . . and suddenly he got the inspiration for the greatest work of art in the history of the world. Possessing not even so much as a pencil or a burnt

match, he dipped his forefinger into the glass of water and began recording this greatest of all inspirations . . . on a paper napkin, with New York tap water as his paint. In a matter of seconds . . . the water had diffused through the paper and the grand design vanished, whereupon the greatest artist in the history of the world slumped to the table and died of a broken heart, and the manager came over, and he thought that here was nothing more than a dead wino with a wet napkin. Now, the question is: Would that have been the greatest work of art in the history of the world?"[4]

Vonnegut goes Wolfe one better, however, in having his narrator die *before* he writes this novel and by having him write it on air!

This double fiction of an omniscent narrator writing in the future for no discernible or possible audience, and of the surprising future inhabitants of the earth, provides many opportunities for Vonnegut to comment on the incredible penchant humans have today for self-destruction. For, looked at objectively, the history of humanity appears dedicated to conceiving of better and better ways to destroy itself, its artifacts, and the planet. In a memorable passage, the narrator recounts, from his perspective of a million years in the future, what humans appear to do best. His incredulous tone reflects "the unbelievability of life as it really is" (PS, p. 297), as humans experience it. What he sees are the large-brained, terribly mobile, inquisitive creatures, whose

> big brains . . . would tell their owners, in effect, "Here is a crazy thing we could actually do, probably, but we would never do it, of course. It's just fun to think about." And then, as though in trances, the people would really do it—have slaves fight each other to the death in the Colosseum, or burn people alive in the public square for holding opinions which were locally unpopular, or build factories whose only purpose was to kill people in industrial quantities, or to blow up whole cities, and on and on (GG p. 266).

Seen by this light, such events and acts are so incredible and so violate good sense, as well as self-interest, as to need a radical explanation. Trout, like a doctor diagnosing the illness of a patient, supplies one: "the only real villain in my story: the oversize human

91

brain" (GG, p. 270). This most objective of all narrators becomes the perfect vehicle for satirizing the mind that delights in devising engines of destruction. For example, in describing an exploding rocket, his incredulity emphasizes not human ingenuity, but lack of human foresight in applying thinking not to the problem of survival, but to the problem of how to destroy things. Rather than moral outrage, he adopts the stance of neutral amazement as he ironically discusses "the collective achievement" represented by this device:

> No single human being could claim credit for that rocket, which was going to work so perfectly. It was the collective achievement of all who had ever put their big brains to work on the problem of how to capture and compress the diffuse violence of which nature was capable, and drop it in relatively small packages on their enemies (GG, p. 189-190.)

He captures the discontinuity between the delight in watching a rocket explode and the violent damage resulting from such an explosion. He also contrasts the incredible creativity of humans with the incredible destructiveness of humans by comparing the meeting of the rocket and its target with human sexual consummation using a deadpan commentary together with a famous quotation from Shakespeare.[5] He begins by recalling the exploding rockets he saw while fighting in Vietnam:

> but no explosion . . . in Vietnam could compare with what happened when that Peruvian rocket put the tip of its nose, that part of its body most richly supplied with exposed nerve endings, into that Ecuadorian radar dish.

Rather than complete the sexual image, he breaks the narration to insert a comment about art in the far future: "No one is interested in sculpture these days. Who could handle a chisel or a welding torch with their flippers or their mouths?"[6] The violent wrench from the sexual imagery of the rocket about to hit its target to the objective statement of the lack of sculpture in the future is comic, breaks the narrative flow, and helps set up yet another comic effect as he continues:

> If there were a monument out here in the islands, though,

celebrating a key event in the past, that would be a good one: the moment of mating, right before the explosion, between the rocket and that radar dish.

He speculates on what might fittingly accompany such a monument, if there was to be one, and suggests a quotation from Shakespeare—not about war, but about love:

Into the lava plinth beneath it these words might be incised, expressing the sentiments of all who had had a hand in the design and manufacture and sale and purchase and launch of the rocket, and of all of whom high explosives were a branch of the entertainment industry:

> . . . 'Tis a consummation
> Devoutly to be wish'd.
> William Shakespeare (1564-1616)(GG 189-190)

Throughout *Galápagos* similar quotations from poets, dramatists and novelists, statesmen and philosophers appear set against the picture of the downward slide of humanity into the sea caused by its inability to listen to the wisdom contained in the words of the wise, and by its insistence on following the path of destruction. In this way Vonnegut creates wonderful comic effects, while pointing out human shortcomings and failures, and warning against the approaching disaster.

As Brian Aldiss says in *The Trillion Year Spree*, *Galápagos* is "Sprightly, funny, suspenseful, Candide-like, and endearingly ingenious in its telling, . . . the best SF novel of its year . . .." Elsewhere he exclaims: " . . . the book's a joy."[7] Like *Bluebeard*, *Galápagos* is also the kind of novel that only a mature writer could write well: one who observed widely what humans do, reflected long on what consolation might exist for human shortsightedness and stupidity, and who experienced the tragic joy of life. In contrast to *Cat's Cradle*, which concludes with the world coming to an end and which reflects Bokonon's belief that "Maturity . . . is a bitter disappointment for which no remedy exists, unless laughter can be said to remedy anything" (CC, p. 134), *Galápagos* suggests that laughter and good humor may yet enable us to survive the "bitter disappointment" of our inevitable discovery that the world, humanity, and, yes, we ourselves are not only imperfect, but are also an endangered species. When asked what his avocation was, Bokonon wrote: "'Being alive'"; when asked what his occupation was, he wrote: "'Being dead'" (CC, p. 95). *Galápagos* emphasizes the importance of having an "avocation," rather than only concentrating upon the inevitable human "occupation."

Both *Galápagos*, despite its disaster scenerio, and *Bluebeard*, despite the many defeats and short-comings of its hero, carry with them an air of optimism and joy. Rabo Karabekian, whose mother survived the great massacre of the Armenians by the Turks, which added the word "genocide" to the languages of the world (BB, p. 3), lives to witness the end of the most destructive war yet fought on European soil, where a megalomaniac again introduced genocide in his attempt to systematically exterminate a portion of the human race. *Bluebeard* suggests that through self-acceptance and the serious use of the human imagination, people can become reconciled to the weakness and the fragility of themselves and all humanity, while still remaining outraged at human stupidity and greed and all the disasterous schemes that these "big brained" creatures concoct and then attempt to follow.

Bluebeard offers serious, compelling insights into what is tragic and timeless using a deceptively simple style. Circe Berman, in *Bluebeard*, speaks for many critics and reviewers when she asks Rabo Karabekian: "'How come you never use semicolons?' . . . 'How come you chop it all up into little sections instead of letting it flow and flow?'" (BB, p 38). Karabekian does not deign to give a reason, nor does Vonnegut. Almost all his books, including *Galápagos* and *Bluebeard*, are "written" by narrators who are rank amateurs, single-book authors with no previous writing experience, and hence the "telegraphic . . . manner of [their] tales" is as appropriate for them as it was for the Tralfamadoreans in *Slaughterhouse-Five*. Peter Nichols, in his favorable review of *Bluebeard*, connected Vonnegut's choppy style to his penchant for self-caricature and identified it as a source of his jocularity but then went on to complain that it was also "disfigured by nervous tics."[8] Still, Vonnegut's simple style remains his strategic choice. Evolving over time and through the writing of many novels, it allows him to communicate readily with a wide audience, as if he were telling the story in person. He, himself, sees it as a positive accomplishment: "Thoreau, I now feel," he says, "wrote in the voice of a child, as do I" (P.S. p. 58). Perhaps, too, the best way of answering such objections is to agree with the scholar and writer, C. S. Lewis, who admonished another generation of readers: "A man ought not to be ashamed of reading a good book because it is simple and popular."[9]

Bluebeard's hero, Rabo Karabekian, is the Abstract Expressionist painter last seen at the Midland City Arts Festival in *Breakfast of Champions*. His painting, *The Temptation of St. Anthony*, together with a Henry Moore sculpture, were the first—and it would turn out, the only—two pieces in the collection of the Mildred Barry Memorial Arts Center. Before the Arts Festival begins, Karabekian is challenged by a cocktail waitress about the value of his painting. It had cost the Center fifty-thousand dollars and, like all Abstract Expression Art, it did not appear to refer very directly to its subject, if it referred to it at all: It "was twenty feet wide and sixteen feet high. The field was *Hawaiian Avocado*, a green wall paint . . . [with a single] vertical stripe [of] . . . dayglo orange reflecting tape" (BC, p. 208). Not much for fifty-thousand dollars. But Karabekian gives a spirited defense of his work:

> " . . . the picture your city owns shows everything about life which truly matters, with nothing left out. It is a picture of the awareness of every animal. It is the immaterial core of every animal—the 'I am' to which all messages are sent. It is all that is alive in any of us—in a mouse, in a deer, in a cocktail waitress. It is unwavering and pure, no matter what preposterous adventure may befall us. A sacred picture of St. Anthony alone is one vertical, unwavering band of light. If a cockroach were near him, or a cocktail waitress, the picture would show two such bands of light. Our awareness of all that is alive and maybe sacred in any of us. Everything else about us is dead machinery. . . . Citizens of Midland city, I salute you . . .. You have given a home to a masterpiece!" (BC, p. 221).

Besides its self-confidence what is striking about Karabekian's statement, what it shares with much of contemporary theorizing about modern art, is that it bears little relation to the content of the painting because, in fact, the painting has no content. It is simply a vertical band of dayglo orange on a green field. No longer is beauty in the eye of the beholder, but artistic significance is wholly within the head of the observer who theorizes. Such speculations, as Karabekian's, led Tom Wolfe to write his spirited, if highly opinionated, book about theory and modern art, *The Painted Word*.[10]

Bluebeard raises the issue of who is a "real" artist by juxtaposing the Abstract Expressionist painters, including Karabekian, to the illustrator, Dan Gregory who paints things more real than they appear to the eye, and who lords it over the non-representational painters and those whose works are housed in the Museum of Modern Art in New York City.[11] The public wants what Gregory has to offer, thus making him enormously wealthy, "probably the highest paid artist in American history" (BB, p. 50). Although famous, much of what he paints can be classified as "merely decorative"[12]; that is, it may be meticulously painted, but it has no emotional or spiritual content. Its purpose is simply to illustrate in a magazine someone else's ideas or someone else's feelings: it is "good painting about nothing."[13] His paintings, although painted in minute and exact detail, are, therefore, as void of content as are Rabo Karabekian's extremely well-executed huge canvasses. So the question arises: Are Dan Gregory's fantastic illustrations and Jackson Pollock's poured paintings or Terry Kitchen's spray gun paintings equally valuable or equally trivial? Or is each just one person's attempt to play with paint? How do each of the three measure up against the great artists of other ages? Do we move in some fashion from Rembrandt to Pollock?[14] Or from Gregory to Karabekian?

Vonnegut gives a subtle and complex answer to these questions. He examines the Abstract Expressionists, as represented by Karabekian's and others' exuberant splashing of paint on canvas, and after looking at the astronomical prices paid for such splashing, he smiles and comments wryly: "Tastes change."[15] Within the novel, the form artistic justice takes is to have Karabekian's paintings return, "thanks to unforeseen chemical reactions," after a period of time to their pristine state as sized canvas: ". . . people who had paid fifteen- or twenty- or even thirty thousand [sic] dollars for a picture . . . found themselves gazing at a blank canvas, all ready for a new picture, and ringlets of colored tapes and what looked like moldy Rice Krispies on the floor (BB, p. 19).[16] "Now you see it, now you don't," as stage magicians used to say during the Great Depression.

The positive alternative *Bluebeard* suggests, to these various kinds of contentless paintings, is seen in Karabekian's final canvas, "Now It's the Women's Turn." His last work, hidden from everyone until the very end of his life, is not an Abstract Expressionist composition, nor is it, although it may appear to be, a literal illustration. His subject is the moment when World War II ended in Europe; his execution is exact to the minutest detail. Looking at the emormous sixty-four-by-eight-foot canvas, an observer feels, correctly, that each of the hundreds, the thousands of miniscule characters in this huge painting has a story. Ironically, the 5,219 figures in the painting are so convincingly real precisely because the artist invented the war story of each of them "and then painted the person it had happened to"! (BB, p. 283).

"In the land of the blind, the one-eyed man is king," runs the ancient proverb, and Karabekian, the one-eyed painter, is indeed king in the land of art: with this last painting, this "last thing I have to give to the world," he discovers and fulfills his vocation as an artist, something he had been unable to do either as an Abstract Expressionist or as an illustrator. Unlike his earlier work, his last monumental painting reflects his life-experience, his feelings, and gives him peace, while exciting the common people who come to view it (BB, pp. 300, 283). Karabekian himself observed the setting of his painting "when the sun came up the day the Second World War ended in Europe" (BB, p. 281), but the meaning, the significance of this event, only revealed itself to him over time, as the meaning or non-meaning of Dresden unfolded itself over time to Vonnegut.

Vonnegut thus suggests that the true artist will use technique in the service of human beings and their human feelings. He thereby alligns himself with painters such as Adolph Gottlieb and Mark Rothko, who in an important statement printed in the column of Edward Alden Jewell, art critic, *The New York Times*, on 13 June 1943 challenged the "widely accepted notion among painters that it does not matter what one paints as long as it is well painted. This is the essence of academism." They maintained as a positive alternative that "There is no such thing as good painting about nothing. We assert

97

that the subject is crucial and only subject-matter is valid which is tragic and timeless. . . . Consequently, if our work embodies these beliefs it must insult any one who is spiritually attuned to interior decoration; pictures for the home . . . ."[17] In the end Karabekian serves humanity not by providing it with more interior or exterior decoration, but by depicting a "crucial [subject]. . . which is tragic and timeless." In so doing, he stands out in bold relief against the pale shadow of Dan Gregory, who, despite all his talent, remained during his whole life, only a "decorator"—an illustrator working for pay, able to reproduce anything for anyone.[18]

 Bluebeard, like *Slaughterhouse-Five*, ends with a vision of accepting life as it is, but with a significant difference: if *Slaughterhouse-Five* left readers with a vision of Tralfamadorian serenity—which by definition is extra-terrestial, hence unattainable by human beings—*Bluebeard* leaves readers with the acceptance of human limits, whether of artists, friends or parents. In Karabekian's last momumental painting, readers see all of life, including lunatics, war prisoners, concentration camp victims, the ragged remants of an exhausted army, and civilians—the dead, dying, and living. Here is all humanity as the sun comes up after the disaster. Gone is the wornout world of the war. "Now It's The Women's Turn," and perhaps they will manage things better. Surely, says Vonnegut at the end of this, his twelfth novel, it is time for a new beginning.

NOTES

1 "All fiction is metaphor. Science fiction is a metaphor. . . . The future, in fiction, is a metaphor." Ursula K. Le Guin, *The Left Hand of Darkness* (New York: Ace, 1969, "Introduction," 1976), n.p.

2 See the discussion of *Cat's Cradle*, pp. 44-49.

3 Vonnegut has become increasingly worried about human destruction of the natural world and, even worse, of human ignorance of nature that encourages such destruction. Faced with a choice between comfort and machine entertainment and some discomfort and the natural world, most people will choose the machine; see *Player Piano*, "Deer in the Works," *Breakfast of Champions*, and *Galápagos*.

4 *The Painted Word* (New York: Farrar, Straus & Giroux, 1975), reprint (New York: Bantam, 1976), pp. 103-104. Compare Rabo Karabekian's disappearing paintings which might as well have been painted with tapwater or Kilgore Trout's inability to find any writing implement in *Breakfast of Champions* (p. 67).

5 Vonnegut's deadpan narration is worthy of the comedian, Jack Benny, the master of the deadpan delivery and the double-take whom Vonnegut listened to Sunday nights during the Great Depression; see Robert Scholes, "A Talk with Kurt Vonnegut, Jr.," *The Vonnegut Statement,* ed. Jerome Klinkowitz and John Somer (New York: Dell, 1973), p. 109.

6 Trout-Vonnegut is playing games with readers' expectations: raising and then deliberately thwarting them in much the same way that Laurence Sterne toyed with his reader in his novels.

7 *The Trillion Year Spree* (New York: Atheneum, 1986), p. 329; and letter to the author from Brian W. Aldiss, 14 November 1988.

8 Book review given over the BBC World Service, May 5, 1988.

9 C. S. Lewis, "High and Low Brows," quoted by Brian W. Aldiss, "Was Zilla Right?: Fantasy and Truth," *Journal of the Fantastic in the Arts,* I. 1 (1988), p. 9.

10 Unlike Wolfe, Vonnegut provides an example of a positive, genuinely artistic achievement in Karabekian's last painting.

11 Ironically, for a follower of Mussolini, Gregory's postion on non-representational art is remarkably similar to the official Stalinist one. See: Vladimir Kemenov, "Aspects of Two Cultures," in *VOKS Bulletin* (Moscow), USSR Society for Cultural Relations with Foreign Countries, 1947, pp. 20-36, who argues that "The basic features of decadent bourgeois art are its falseness, its belligerent anti-realism, its hostility to objective knowledge and to the truthful portrayal of life in art." He goes on to say that art must follow "the path of socialist realism, a path pointed out by Stalin." Reprinted in Herchel B. Chipp, *Theories of Modern Art* (Berkeley: University of California Press, 1968), pp. 490, 495.

12 From Holger Cahill, "The Federal Art Project": "Surely art is not merely decorative, a sort of unrelated accompaniment to life. In a genuine sense it should have use; it should be interwoven with the very stuff and texture of human experience, intensifying that experience, making it more profound, rich, clear, and coherent. This can be accomplished only if the artist is functioning freely in relation to society, and if society wants what he is able to offer." From *New Horizons in American Art* (New York: The Museum of Modern Art, 1936), in Chipp, p. 473.

13 Adolph Gottlieb and Mark Rothko, a statement printed in the column of Edward Alden Jewell, art critic, *The New York Times,* 13 June 1943: "There is no such thing as good painting about nothing." Quoted in Chipp, p. 545; see also n.16.

14 Although grouping some of the moderns with the Great Masters may appear either strained or pure errant nonsense, depending upon one's view of the moderns, at least one critic lumped them all together or, rather, in his inelegant prose, "tossed [them] into one pot": "The pictures of de Kooning and Kline, it seemed to me, were suddenly tossed into one pot with Rembrandt and Giotto. All alike became painters of illusion."! Leo Steinburg quoted in Wolfe, p. 79.

15 Jacket blurb written and signed by Vonnegut, 1 April 1987 for the hardcover edition of *Bluebeard*.

16 Karabekian is an early example of a Conceptualist painter, one whose work exists only as a concept. See the story, "The Greatest Artist in the History of the World," pages 90-9 above. The trade name of the disappearing paint changes from *Breakfast of Champions* to *Bluebeard*, as casually as the names of characters shift between and among stories and novels. Vonnegut says several times that such changes have no significance; see, for example: Reilly, "Two Conversations with Kurt Vonnegut," pp. 7-8.

17 Chipp, p. 545.

18 The ultimate move in this direction may have occurred "the day he [Andy Warhol] put an ad in *The Village Voice* saying he would endorse anything, anything at all, for money . . . and listing his telephone number" (Wolfe, p. 86).

VIII. Upbeat and Slick:
the Short Fiction in
Welcome to the Monkey House

Vonnegut began his career writing short stories weekends while working in public relations for the General Electric Research Laboratory in Schenectady, New York. He sent his first story, "Report on the Barnhouse Effect," to *Collier's* magazine whose fiction editor, Knox Burger, liked it, thought the then-unknown writer showed promise, but also believed that the story lacked an ending. Starting from this point, Vonnegut tells two different versions of what happened: either Burger himself "told ... what was wrong with it and how to fix it" (PS, p. 113) or his agent, Kenneth Littauer, actually wrote the missing ending for him.[1] But whomever may deserve credit for the ending, the point is that, although he was only an unknown if promising writer, Vonnegut still received the kind of professional help and sound advice he needed to succeed in what was then a highly competitive market. He gratefully took both the help and advice, with the result that he sold "the story for seven hundred and fifty dollars, six weeks' pay at G.E." (PS, p. 113). He then sat down and wrote another which he also sent to Burger who "paid me nine hundred [sic] and fifty dollars, and suggested that it was perhaps time for me to quit G.E. Which I did" (PS, p. 113).

In successfully launching his career as a writer, Vonnegut fulfilled one of his mother's dreams of becoming rich by publishing fiction in the magazines:

> After our family lost almost all of its money in the Great Depression, my mother thought she might make a new fortune by writing for the slick magazines. She took short story courses at night. She studied magazines the way gamblers study racing forms. ... when I grew up, I was able to make her dream come true (PS, pp. 95-97).

Magazine writing paid so well that Vonnegut stuck to it and therefore did not write his second novel until almost eight years after *Player Piano* was published. "Eventually," he says somewhat bemused by it all, "my price for a short story got up to twenty-nine hundred dollars a crack. Think of that" (PS, p. 113). Small wonder that he concentrated on selling his short stories to the so-called "slick" magazines, such as *Collier's, The Saturday Evening Post, Cosmopolitan,* and *The Ladies Home Journal,* while "scrambling to make a living without a regular job" working at an advertising agency and, even, selling Saabs. (He and a partner had the second Saab dealership in the United States.)[2]

His short fiction collected first in *Canary in a Cathouse* (1961)— no longer available—was mostly reprinted in *Welcome to the Monkey House* (1968), which includes all but one story from the earlier collection. During his career as a short-story writer, Vonnegut published other stories, but these are the ones he has chosen rightfully to preserve, while discarding others that were clearly apprentice work. Joe David Bellamy correctly asserts that *"Welcome to the Monkey House* gives perhaps the clearest perspective on this [Vonnegut's as writer] growth, for in almost every case the more recent stories are the all-around better stories; the title story, the best in the collection, is the most recent of all."[3]

All of the stories he chose for inclusion in this collection, entertain, most amuse, while a few challenge commonly held assumptions and values. Usually the good hero will "win" in some sense, unlike in his novels where at the end most of the heroes are either dead or about to die. The two exceptions, Eliot Rosewater in *God Bless You, Mr. Rosewater* and Rudy Waltz in *Deadeye Dick,* are not dead, but neither are they fully functioning human beings: Eliot, looking like "F. Scott Fitzgerald with one day to live," is confined to an insane asylum (GB, p. 182), while Rudy, who calls himself a "neuter" and is a double murderer, has never really lived.

Vonnegut's very first story, which launched his professional writing career, "Report on the Barnhouse Effect" (1950), contains elements that became staples in his future novels: a lone man working on a strange idea makes an important discovery that can change the world for the worst (compare *Cat's Cradle, The Sirens of Titan* or *Player Piano*) or the better (compare *God Bless You, Mr. Rosewater, Slapstick* and, possibly, *Galápagos*). To have things turn out "right," he must resist the blandishments of "the nation's political and military great" (WMH, p. 169; compare *Cat's Cradle* where the three

Hoenikker children under similar circumstances succumb easily to temptation) and must also turn his back on any dream of personal fame or fortune (compare *Mother Night, God Bless You, Mr. Rosewater* and *Bluebeard*). He must trust himself because he knows what is right and knows it better than those in positions of power who possess the "received wisdom." In the short story, Barnhouse's appeal to a human "conscience" to approve his attempt to disarm the world illustrates the humane values that underlie almost all the novels (WMH, p. 173) and that guide Vonnegut himself as a writer with a "conscience." Barnhouse also knows that his knowledge could be perverted into a popular religion, which does happen in *Player Piano, The Sirens of Titan, Cat's Cradle, Slapstick*, and *Galápagos*. Finally this story, like so many of Vonnegut's stories and novels, uses colloquial language and common speech to help win readers' trust and confidence in a narrator who appears to be "just like us."

The stories overall, including this first published one, are positive and definitely "upbeat" because, as Vonnegut says, that's what the magazines they were written for demanded and "business is business."[4] Even "Manned Missiles" (1958) is, on balance, "upbeat." That story focuses on a disaster in space as told through the touching correspondence of an American father with a Russian father, both of whom mourn their sons killed when their spaceships collided.

All of the stories are a far cry from the cynicism or pessimism that characterizes most of the early novels. The faceless horrors of an automated industrial plant built on an inhuman scale found in *Player Piano*, for instance, also occur in "Deer in the Works" (1955), which is similarly set in Illium. In the novel, however, the abortive revolution leads to mindless destruction while in the end the forces of repression regain their power. In contrast, the deer in the story—itself a symbol of vitality, freedom, pride and nature—successfully gains its release. The price it pays for being in the maze-like "Works" and encountering men and machines, however, includes dirt—it is "streaked with soot and grease"—and broken antlers. The human protagonist also wisely "didn't look back" as he follows the deer and heads for the woods himself, thus choosing the freedom offered by nature and the greater security found in a world constructed on a human scale, over the promise of financial security in the "Works" (WMH, p. 220-221).

Another theme common to both novel and story is humanity against machines. In the story, "EPICAC" (1950), a computer blows its fuses over not being human and therefore not being able to love. Its last printed words are "I don't want to be a machine, and I don't want to think about war. I want [to be human]," which is impossible, so it self-destructs leaving a suicide note and hundreds of love poems behind (WMH, p. 284). In contrast the machine, Checker Charlie, in *Player Piano*, fails not because of having an inferiority complex, but because of human error. In the championship checker match of Checker Charlie versus the hero Paul Proteus, Checker Charlie erupts in flames, which destroy its circuits. It loses the match not because it despairs of becoming human, but because a human being incorrectly wired it. Its defeat is not a defeat for machines or automation, since all the actual power in the United States still rests with the formidable EPICAC XIV that runs everything, is "dead right about everything" (PP, p. 116), and ultimately controls everyone in the country from its lair in the Carlsbad Caverns in Colorado. There it continues to run smoothly, untouched by anything human including the abortive Illium rebellion.

Of the two stories that warn of the dangers of overpopulation, the collection's title story, "Welcome to the Monkey House" (1968), and the much earlier "Tomorrow and Tomorrow and Tomorrow" (1953) are both on balance positive, which contrasts with the Kilgore Trout story on the same subject incorporated into *God Bless You, Mr. Rosewater*. In Trout's story, "2BRO2B" (GB, pp. 20-21), the Ethical Suicide Parlors are a last despairing resort, and his story concludes with a customer's cry, "What in hell are people *for?*" "Welcome to the Monkey House," on the other hand, after describing a similar over-crowded world, concludes with the hero successfully subverting the official anti-feeling, anti-life forces in favor of life, love, sex, and humanity. Vonnegut says he wrote this story "on assignment" from *Playboy* magazine, which suggested the plot based upon his earlier novel. It is clearly better crafted than the other stories in the collection showing the results of Vonnegut's appreticeship in writing dozens of stories and six novels. At the end of "Tomorrow and Tomorrow and Tomorrow," written fifteen years earlier, most of the characters, who in the beginning of the story complained bitterly about the over-crowded conditions in which they were forced to live because of overpopulation in 2158 A.D., now enjoy more space than they have ever had to live in before either because they find themselves in a jail cell that is far more spacious than their living quarters or they are left in their now-deserted flat with the rest of the family in jail. Gramps, the main character, subbornly refuses to die to make available more physical space for the younger generation. Instead, he continues to live even happier than before: "He could hardly wait to see what was going to happen next" (WMH, p. 308).

As in "Welcome to the Monkey House," the central idea in "Harrison Bergeron" (1961) of forcing people to become equal through applying handicaps was also derived from an earlier novel, *The Sirens of Titan*. In the novel the system of handicaps is, however, only incidental to the founding of the Church of God the Utterly Indifferent, whereas it is at the very center of the story which concludes with the hero's suicidal challenge to the grotesque system. For an instant Bergeron succeeds, as freed from his handicaps and united with the equally brave dancer "in an explosion of joy and grace, into the air they sprang!" (WMH, p. 12). But unlike most of Vonnegut's tales, this bold act changes little or nothing as both Bergeron and the dancer are brutally killed as they leap. Not even Harrison's parents, who witness his death on their home tv screen, are able to acknowledge either his triumphant rebellion or his subsequent death, except in the most trivialized act of appearing as "Something real sad on television," so powerful is the forceful distraction produced by their own handicaps (WMH, p. 13). This far from upbeat ending is a distinct exception in Vonnegut's stories.

Magazines also welcomed Vonnegut's well-written, albeit mostly predictable, stories of love conquering all obstacles, such as "A Long Walk to Forever" (1950), "Go Back to Your Precious Wife and Son" (1962), as well as the slightly fantastic, "Next Door" (1955). In several other equally positive stories, people are able to live out their fantasies, as in "Who Am I This Time?" (1961) where two lovers reenact the great love affairs of all time through acting together in plays produced by a community theatre;[5] or in "The Foster Portfolio" (1951) where George Foster ignores his accumulating wealth in favor of fulfilling his dream "to play piano in a dive, and breathe smoke, and drink gin, to be Firehouse Harris, his father's son, three nights out of seven" (WMH, p. 69); or in "More Stately Mansion" (1951) where a woman lives in fantasy so completely that she does not notice when it becomes transformed into reality! Occasionally a story uses fantasy simply to amuse and entertain. In "Tom Edison's Shaggy Dog" (1953), for example, an intelligent dog helps Edison invent the lightbulb, while in "Unready to Wear" (1953) people learn how to do without bodies, and in "The Euphio Question" (1951) the world is threatened by euphoria being broadcast from outer space.

In the early fifties, Vonnegut sold a series of "human interest" stories to *The Saturday Evening Post* centering on George Hemholtz, a high school bandmaster and teacher who would confront a difficult problem and through determination and empathy solve it.[6] (Helmholtz also appears as a very minor character in *The Sirens of Titan*.) In the only one of these stories included in this collection, "The Kid Nobody Could Handle" (1955), Helmholtz encounters a boy deaf and blind to common humanity "without fear, without dreams, without love" (WMH, p. 259), who "can't feel anything" (WMH, p. 262), and who is bent on destroying anything good or beautiful or valuable to someone else. Helmholtz finds a way, through sacrificing his most valuable possession, to reach the young man and save him from himself. "Our aim," he concludes, "is to make the world more beautiful than it was when we came into it. It can be done. You can do it" (WMH, p. 263)—which is almost a motto for all of these stories with very few exceptions.

At the center of one of those exceptions, "The Lie" (1962), a father and son must confront their personal failure. In this tale well-meaning parents unreasonably place the burden of their hopes and values on their young son. When he proves unable to meet their expectations by failing to pass the entrance exams required for admission to the prepschool his father and grandfather had attended and subsequently richly endowed, he becomes in turn unable to face his parents' disappointment in him, so he lies about both his disappointing test results and his subsequent rejection by the school. When his father discovers the truth, he, too, proves unable to bear its burden and so makes a "lie" out of his own first principle in life, which is never to ask for special treatment just because the family has endowed so many of the school's buildings and programs. When it becomes known to other parents and students that the father has indeed asked for an exception to be made in his son's behalf, both parents and child are left completely isolated by others. If there is any consolation for them, it lies in their coming together in their suffering as parents and child. At best, this is but a bittersweet ending. Similarly, the ending of "D.P." (1953) suggests that all does not always end well despite the absence of villains and the presence of good will by everyone involved. A war orphan "displaced" in a Germany institution escapes for a day and goes in search of his father among a U.S. army unit he happens to meet. Too young to understand the forces arrayed against him, he accepts on face value a soldier's promise to return and take him "back home across the water" (WMH, p. 161)—a promise given in desperation by a service man grief-stricken over the plight of the boy, but also aware that the child must for his own sake agree to return peacefully to the orphanage.

The war also forms the backdrop against which Vonnegut tells two other stories equally moving emotionally: In one of his finest tales, "All the King's Horses" (1953), an American colonel, forced to play chess with a guerrilla chief for the lives of his company and family, at first loses, then, eventually regains his confidence with the result that he wins the game and rescues his comrades. In "Adam" (1954), a well-told tale of two survivors of the death camps, the birth of a long-awaited child becomes a miracle that affirms their lives as a gift, despite the horrors of war, the prosaic setting in which they find themselves currently, and the blasé reactions of those around them (WMH, pp. 285-92).

Later, in *Jailbird*, Vonnegut will return to the concentration camp survivor as parent but will do so from a diametrically opposed viewpoint. Gone from the novel is the story's optimism and poignancy, and in their places is a truly forelorn hopelessness. Ruth, the narrator's wife, survived the Nazi atrocities but at the price of losing all hope. She says later that she "feels that it would be just as well if nobody had babies anymore, if the human race did not go on" (JB, p. 68). She adds, "If I had one, it would be a monster" upon which her husband, years later and with the advantage of hindsight, comments: "And it came to pass" (JB, p. 69). Her opinion of the Nazi death camps and those who designed, built, and staffed them is as scathing as it is specific. It would be completely out of place in Vonnegut's short fiction, which rarely admits complexity, ambiguity or tragedy. Ruth raises for readers the complicated issue of human intelligence in the service of pure hatred and death, instead, as in the stories, of love and life: "my wife Ruth, the Ophelia of the death camps," says Walter J. Starbuck: "... believed that ... It was thinkers, after all, who had set up the death camps. Setting up a death camp, with its railroad sidings and its around-the-clock crematoria, was not something a moron could do" (JB, p. 195). Nor do the stories feature complicated, if understated emotion, such as Starbuck's final comment on Ruth's opinion of those who dedicated themselves to attempting to extinguish a portion of the human race that they judged "non-human": "Neither could a moron explain why a death camp was ultimately humane" (JB, p. 195).

In contrast to the novels, all the stories in *Welcome to the Monkey House*, with the exception of "D.P." and possibly "The Lie," have relatively happy endings. Though it is true some people do die in "All the King's Horses" and there is the price to be paid in loss of self-respect in "The Lie" and George Helmholtz does have to sacrifice his most loved possession to carry the day in "The Kid Nobody Could Handle," they too appear to show that people can "make the world more beautiful than it was when [they] . . . came into it." These last four stories begin to suggest the complexity of human beings and the situations in which people often find themselves, but such complexity is rare in Vonnegut's short fiction.

With the disappearance of the magazine market in the late fifties, Vonnegut was forced to devote all his time to novel writing. The choice proved a happy one, for his novels are far better than any of his stories. It was as if he needed the room novels gave him to stretch out: to deepen his characters, to try out stylistic effects over a couple hundred pages, and to follow where his "conscience" would lead him artistically.

NOTES

1 "Kurt Vonnegut," *The Writer's Workshop*, SCTV-PBS, 1980.
2 Ibid.
3 "Kurt Vonnegut for President: the Making of an Academic Reputation," in *The Vonnegut Statement* ed. Jerome Klinkowitz and John Somer (New York: Dell, 1973), p. 78.
4 Quoted in Stanley Schatt, *Kurt Vonnegut, Jr.* (Boston: G. K. Hall, 1976), p. 119.

5 Vonnegut uses this motif in *Deadeye Dick* where Celia Hoover confesses to Rudy Waltz: "That play of yours—changed my life. . . . All those wonderful words that came out of me—those were your words. I could never have thought up words that beautiful to say in a million years. I almost lived and died without ever saying anything worth listening to" (DD, pp. 179-180).

6 Schatt, pp. 127-128.

IX. Primary Bibliography

Because this Guide is designed for the general reader of Vonnegut, all references in the text except for WF&G are to Dell mass-market paperbacks, the most widely available edition. (More reliable are the uniform hardback editions issued by Seymore Lawrence/Delacorte Press.) Both the dates of first editions and mass market paperback editions are given in this bibliography.

Between Time and Timbuktu or Prometheus-5. New York: Delacorte Press, 1972; Dell, 1973. A montage by David O'Dell of Vonnegut's early novels and WJ, including plots, characters, and themes. Includes material contributed and performed by Bob Elliot and Ray Goulding, two of Vonnegut's favorite comedians.

Bluebeard. New York: Delacorte Press, 1987; Dell, 1988. The fictional autobiography of the Abstract Expressionist painter, Rabo Karabekian, whose mother survived the great massacre of the Armenians and who himself witnessed the end of the Second World War and lived to paint it. Asks "who or what is the true artist?" while examining the need for self-acceptance and forgiveness in living a good life.

Breakfast of Champions. New York: Delacorte Press; 1973, Dell, 1974. Vonnegut's fantasy of a return to lost innocence; an antic comedy about living beyond the "mid-life crisis" with the author himself as a prominent character told in his best naive style. Kilgore Trout, although still a complete failure as a writer, wins the Nobel Prize for medicine.

Cat's Cradle. New York: Holt, Rinehart & Winston, 1963; Dell, 1965. Vonnegut's excellent comic treatment of humanity's immaturity and apparent willingness to destroy all life on Earth. Includes his most successful satiric religion, Bokononism, as well as the *Books of Bokonon* which are full of *foma* or harmless lies to live by.

Deadeye Dick. New York: Delacorte Press, 1982; Dell, 1985. The quiet lament for the unlived life of Rudy Waltz who commits a murder at twelve years of age, thus effectively ending his own life. A serious examination of the dangerous myths of progress, and the harmlessness of guns and the neutron bomb. Advocates taking responsibility for one's acts.

Galápagos. New York: Delacorte Press, 1985; Dell, 1986. An exuberant comic look at the dubious future of humankind as told "a million years in the future" by Leon Trout, son of Kilgore. Aldiss rightly called it "the best SF novel of its year." The work of a mature writer, it is clearly vintage Vonnegut.

God Bless You, Mr. Rosewater. New York: Holt, Rinehart & Winston, 1965; Dell, 1966. Vonnegut's wrestling with the right use and mysterious nature of money, the implications of the Sermon on the Mount, and the need for disinterested love.

Happy Birthday, Wanda June. New York: Delacorte Press, 1971; Dell,1971. Vonnegut's rewriting of the *Odyssey* using Ernest Hemingway as the hero. Good comic moments; favorably reviewed upon opening in New York.

Jailbird. New York: Delacorte Press, 1979; Dell, 1980. The Watergate novel that views corruption in government against the background of the miscarriage of justice in the Sacco and Vanzetti executions, the "pornography" of labor history, and the destruction of the planet Earth. Money does not help much here nor does the failure to take adult responsibilities seriously. Memorable characters include the shopping bag lady, Mary Kathleen O'Looney and Bob Fender, the new identity of Kilgore Trout.

Mother Night. Greenwich, CT: Fawcett, 1961; New York: Harper & Row, 1966 (includes the now standard introduction); Dell, 1974. An inventive novel that takes a long, sober look at the schizophrenic personality, and the dangers of collaborating with evil.

Palm Sunday: An Autobiographical Collage. New York: Delacorte Press, 1981; Dell, 1984. An unusually revealing collection of personal pieces about Vonnegut's life, family, opinions, and beliefs. Provides one of the best contexts within which to read his fiction.

Player Piano. New York: Charles Scribner's Sons, 1952; Dell, 1974. Vonnegut's first novel based upon his experience working for General Electric Research Laboratory and warning against the dangers of meaningless work in the coming age of automation.

The Sirens of Titan. New York: Dell, 1959. An incredibly inventive tour of the solar system with some of Vonnegut's most memorable characters and creations. History offers no consolation for human suffering. This novel has withstood the test of time very well.

Slapstick or Lonesome No More!. New York, Delacorte Press, 1976; Dell, 1978. Fantastic tale of overcoming American loneliness by the President establishing extended families for everyone. Fluctuating gravity forces humans to stop relying on most machines.

Slaughterhouse-Five or The Children's Crusade. New York: Delacorte Press, 1969; Dell, 1971. The most famous and most successful of Vonnegut novels, which wrestles with the issues of unmotivated human suffering and the power of evil in the world.

Wampeters, Foma & Granfaloons. New York: Delacorte Press, 1974; Dell, 1976. A revealing collection of occasional pieces from 1965-1974 including the *Playboy* interview, much of his personal journalism, and several important public addresses.

Welcome to the Monkey House. New York: Delacorte Press, 1968; Dell, 1970. Contains all the stories from 1950 to 1968 that Vonnegut wishes to preserve including all but one ("Hal Irwin's Magic Lamp"), originally published in *Canary in a Cat House* (1961). Most stories reflect the taste of the slick magazine audience for which they were written, and all are "upbeat."

(with Ivan Chermayeff). *Sun, Moon, Star.* New York: Harper & Row, 1980. Children's book created by Vonnegut arranging and captioning the various bright, abstract designs by artist Chermayeff.

"A Talk with Kurt Vonnegut, Jr." with Robert Scholes. *The Vonnegut Statement.* Ed. Jerome Klinkowitz and John Somer. New York: Delacorte and Dell, 1973. pp. 90-118. A talk that took place at the University of Iowa while Vonnegut was teaching at the University of Iowa Writers' Workshop. Scholes and Vonnegut exchange quips about the Depression, radio comedians, and the background of his novels. Many ideas and expressions used here for the first time turn up in numerous subsequent interviews.

"Interview" with John Casey and Joe David Bellamy in *The New Fiction.* Ed. Joe David Bellamy. Urbana: University of Illinois Press, 1974. pp. 194-207.

Kurt Vonnegut, Jr: The Novelist Talks about His Life and Work with John Disney. Audio-Text Cassette, The Center for Cassette Studies, Inc., North Hollywood, CA, CBC758, 1970. Interviewed in his Cape Cod home, Vonnegut talks with a group of young people giving his views on the role of the writer in contemporary society while discussing his work through *Slaughterhouse-Five.*

"Two Conversations with Kurt Vonnegut" with Charlie Reilly. *College Literature* 7.1 (Winter 1980), pp. 1-29. A revealing, wide-ranging discussion of Vonnegut's life and times together with some talk about the fiction.

"Vonnegut Is Having Fun Doing a Play" with Mel Gussow. *The New York Times*, 6 October 1970, p. 56. Vonnegut discusses the New York production of *Happy Birthday, Wanda June,* and tells of his plans to write more plays and fewer novels.

Writer's Workshop. SCTV, PBS, 1980. Televised interview in which Vonnegut offers advice to young writers, while telling them of his life and career.

X. Secondary Bibliography

Abádi-Nagy, Zoltán. "Ironic Historicism in the American Novel of the Sixties." *John O'Hara Journal*, 5.1&2 (Winter 1982-83), pp. 83-89. A concise study of the major novels of the sixties using Vonnegut's "steamroller of history" (MN) as the basic metaphor. Pertinent comments on *The Sirens of Titan, Mother Night* and *Cat's Cradle.*

Barnes, Clive. "Stage: 'Happy Birthday, Wanda June.'" *The New York Times,* 9 October 1970, p. 43. Highly favorable review of opening night.

Berryman, Charles. "After the Fall: Kurt Vonnegut." *Critique* 26 (Winter 1985), pp. 96-102. Article examines the thesis that "Vonnegut has continued after *Slaughterhouse-Five* to explore the images of a haunted memory, but he has produced a very uneven series of novels."

Broer, Lawrence R. *Sanity Plea: Schizophrenia in the Novels of Kurt Vonnegut.* Ann Arbor: UMI Research Press, 1989. A discussion of schizophrenia in Vonnegut's novels through *Bluebeard.* After faulting other critics for misreading the novels, Broer proceeds to undermine his own reading with numerous inaccuracies including "swan's rude slapstick" rather than "man's" in SS (109, 118 cf. SS 230); Terry Kitchens rather than the correct, Kitchen (174); Rabo rather than Jim Brooks (172 cf. BB. 171); Circe did not speak of "The peaceable kingdom," and the "Genesis Gang," but Marilee did, (172, 175 cf. BB 238, 241); Dorothy does not destroy his paintings (163 cf. BB 267). The result is that readers must unfortunately be on their guard against errors instead of evaluating Broer's sometimes provocative interpretations; see especially his Chapter 2 on *The Sirens of Titan.* Highly indebted to Hume's essays.

Giannone, Richard. *Vonnegut: A Preface to His Novels.* Port Washington, NY.: National University Publications, 1977. A lucid analysis of the novels through *Slapstick* against the background of relevant world literature, criticism, and theology. Traces the creation in Vonnegut's works of "a fictive guide to our lost culture."

—. "Violence in the Fiction of Kurt Vonnegut." *Thought*, 56. 220 (March 1981), pp. 62-76. Giannone's thesis is that all of Vonnegut's novels through *Jailbird* form "a sustained response to violence" whether economic, political or military which leads inevitably to "individual stories celebrat[ing] the psychic disorder that chaos is in the human mind." One of the most thoughtful, but deeply pressimistic readings of Vonnegut's work.

Hume, Kathryn. *Fantasy and Mimesis: Responses to Reality in Western Literature*. New York: Methuen, 1984. Provides a context within which to read Vonnegut by documenting the pervasiveness of fantasy within "all but a small part of western literature." Provocative comments on several of Vonnegut's novels, including *Breakfast of Champions, Cat's Cradle, Player Piano, Slaughterhouse-Five* and *The Sirens of Titan*.

—. "Kurt Vonnegut and the Myths and Symbols of Meaning." *Texas Studies in Literature and Language*, 24.4 (Winter 1982), pp. 429-447. There is in Vonnegut ". . . a tension . . . between the pressimism born of experience and the optimism stemming from background and values." Vonnegut presents a "study in the way that experience can adversely effect an artist's ability to use the conventional materials of his culture"—in this case "the hero monomyth, our culture's primary literary structure for conveying an optimistic sense of life's meaning."

—. "Vonnegut's Self-Projections: Symbolic Characters and Symbolic Fiction." *The Journal of Narrative Technique* 12 (Fall 1982), pp.177-90. Hume contends that readers looking for "realism of psychology and of action" have misjudged the unique quality of Vonnegut's writing: "Vonnegut's main characters are usually straightforward projections of some part of his psyche, and they let him work out his inner conflicts." Includes a fresh reading of *Slapstick, Jailbird* and *Breakfast of Champions* plus excellent discussion of the many persona of Kilgore Trout.

Klinkowitz, Jerome. *Kurt Vonnegut*. New York: Methuen, 1982. A discussion of Vonnegut's work through *Jailbird* against the background of cultural change in the United States and the rise of the "new novel." Klinkowitz sees Vonnegut as "a writer simultaneously at the heart of his popular culture and in the forefront of the avant-garde."

— and Donald L. Lawler. *Vonnegut in America.* New York: Delacorte Press, 1977. Essays originally presented at a conference of the Modern Language Association padded out with a useful bibliography, a dozen or so photographs, and less useful, previously published material on Vonnegut's reception in Russia. Worthwhile title essay by Klinkowitz. Bibilography.

— and Somer, John, ed. *The Vonnegut Statement.* New York: Dell, 1973. A collection of original essays on Vonnegut's life, work, and reception. The best of these by James Mellard and John Somer are insightful and important. (See separate listings.)

Leverence, W. John. *"Cat's Cradle* and Traditional American Humor." *Journal of Popular Culture,* 4 (Spring 1972), pp. 955-963. Valuable for its itemization rather than its discussion of Vonnegut's use of humor and comedy in the novel.

Lundquist, James. *Kurt Vonnegut.* New York: Frederick Ungar,1977. A concise informed introduction to Vonnegut through *Slapstick,* which includes a lengthy discussion of science-fiction and Vonnegut's novels.

May, John R. *Toward a New Earth: Apocalypse in the American Novel.* Notre Dame: University of Notre Dame Press, 1972. Clear discussion of *Cat's Cradle* within the context of the apocalyptic strain in American literature. Includes a useful chart: "Typology of Apocalypse."

Mayo, Clark. *Kurt Vonnegut: The Gospel from Outer Space (or, Yes We Have No Nirvanas).* San Bernardino: Borgo , 1977. A clear, concise commentary on Vonnegut's oeuvre through *Slapstick,* which documents the shift from narrator as detached observer in the early novels to involved participant in *Breakfast of Champions* and *Slapstick.*

Mellard, James M. "The Modes of Vonnegut's Fiction: or, *Player Piano* Ousts *Mechanical Bride* and *The Sirens of Titan* Invade *The Gutenberg Galaxy,"* Lawler and Somer. *The Vonnegut Statement,* pp. 178-203. Detailed discussion of *Player Piano* and *The Sirens of Titan* to substantiate the thesis that " . . . Vonnegut moves from a traditional mode, associated with a visual model of the world, to a new mode that begins to recreate an acoustic model."

Merrill, Robert. "Vonnegut's *Breakfast of Champions* and the Conversion of Heliogabalus." *Critique* 18.3 (1979), pp. 41-49. Discusses the interrelatedness of Dwayne Hoover, Kilgore Trout, and the character of Kurt Vonnegut as "exemplary figures in a moral fable" warning us against "the seductions of fatalism."

— and Peter A. Scholl. "Vonnegut's *Slaughterhouse-Five*: The Requirements of Chaos." *Studies in American Fiction* (Spring 1976), pp. 65-76. A clear argument against seeing the novel as a brief for quietism. Tralfamadore is a negative world and Billy Pilgrim is not an Everyman. " . . . what conforts Pilgrim will not do the job for everyone." The Tralfamadore perspective denies "personal responsibility [and] easily leads to the brutal excesses of the Nazis."

Reed, Peter J. *Kurt Vonnegut, Jr.* New York: Thomas Y. Crowell, 1972. A detailed review of the six novels through *Slaughterhouse-Five* including plot summaries and analysis of each.

Schatt, Stanley. *Kurt Vonnegut, Jr.* Boston: G.K. Hall, 1976. A detailed discussion of the novels, stories, and plays through *Slapstick,* includes an analysis of plots, characters, themes, and their continuity in Vonnegut's works.

Scholes, Robert. *Fabulation and Metafiction.* Urbana: University of Illinois Press, 1979. Scholes provides an excellent critical context for reading Vonnegut. Chapters on Vonnegut's college writing for the *Cornell Sun, Cat's Cradle* and *Mother Night,* and a perceptive appreciation of *Slaughterhouse-Five.*

Scholl, Peter A. "Vonnegut's Attack Upon Christendom." *Newsletter of the Conference on Christianity and Literature,* 22.1 (Fall 1972), pp. 5-11. Clear, restrained discussion of Vonnegut's wrestling with moral issues and religious questions. Scholl concludes that Vonnegut retains Christian ethical values while eschewing its theology.

Schulz, Max F. "The Unconfirmed Thesis: Kurt Vonnegut, Black Humor, and Contemporary Art." *Critique: Studies in Modern Fiction* 12.2 (1971), pp. 5-28. An in-depth analysis of *God Bless You, Mr. Rosewater* and *Cat's Cradle* with briefer notes on *Mother Night, Happy Birthday, Wanda June,* and *Slaughterhouse-Five* seen against some of the art, music and intellectual currents of the sixties.

Somer, John. "Geodesic Vonnegut; or, If Buckminster Fuller Wrote Novels." Lawler and Somer. *The Vonnegut Statement*, pp. 221-54. One of the best early analyses of Vonnegut's novels through *Slaughterhouse-Five*. Somer discusses each in turn, compares Vonnegut favorably with Robber-Grillet, attempts to assess the influence of Einstein and Fuller by way of Guy Murchie on his thinking, and conludes with an estimate of his "aesthetic strength and freedom."

Tanner, Tony "The Uncertain Messenger (Kurt Vonnegut, Jr)." *City of Words: American Fiction 1950-1970*. London: Jonathan Cape, 1971. pp. 181-201. A judicious view of the novels through *Slaughterhouse-Five*, especially good on *Cat's Cradle* and *Mother Night*.

Wolfe, G. K. "Vonnegut and the Metaphor of Science Fiction: The Sirens of Titan [sic]." *Journal of Popular Culture*, 4 (Spring 1972), pp. 964-969. A concise analysis of "the manner in which Vonnegut uses science fiction" as well as a discussion of the importance of *The Sirens of Titan* for understanding the later novels.

Index

Abadi-Nagy, Zoltán, 33.

ACLU (American Civil Liberties Union), 30.

"Adam," 107.

Adams, Alice Vonnegut: *See* Alice Vonnegut

Agnew, Spiro, 81, 87n.

Aldiss, Brian, 21n, 88, 93.

"All the King's Horses," 107, 108.

"A Long Walk To Forever," 105.

Apulieus, Lucius: *The Golden Ass*, 12-13.

Atlas, Charles, 47-48.

Auden, W.H., 6.

Barnes, Clive, 59. 72n,.

Barthelme, Donald, 19.

"Bartleby, the Scrivener," 80, 83, 88n.

Battle of the Bulge: Vonnegut taken prisoner by the Germans, 7.

Bellamy, Joe David, 21n, 57n, 102.

Benny, Jack, 99n.

Berkove, Lawrence I., 21n.

Between Time and Timbuktu, 59-60, 72.

"Bickerstaff Papers," 12.

Blake, William, 14.

Bluebeard, 5-7, 11, 17-19, 20, 30, 49, 71, 93-98, 100n, 103; Abstract
    Expressionism, 6, 95-97; acceptance of life, 30, 98; illustration, 96-
    98; "Now It's the Women's Turn," 97-98; style, 94-95; *The Temp-
    tation of St. Anthony*, 95-96.

Blume, Judy, 30n.

Bob and Ray, 87n. *See also* Elliot, Bob; Goulding, Ray

Bonhoeffer, Dietrich, 15, 21n.

Borges, Jorge Luis, 19.

Breakfast of Champions, 5-6, 9, 20, 30, 60-67, 70-71, 75, 89, 95, 98n,
    100n; antic novel, 62; innocence of, 65-66; mid-life crisis in, 60-
    61; narrator of, 12, 62, 71; pollution, 62, 65, 66, 89, 98n; racism,
    62-65; style, of 61-64; suicide, 61, 63, 66; Trout, Kilgore, 64-66, 75;
    Nobel Prize in medicine, 75.

Brecht, Bertolt, 25.
Broer, Lawrence R., 88n.
Brothers Karamazov, The, 28.
Bulletin of the Atomic Scientists, 45.
Bunyan, John, 37.
Burger, Knox, 101.

Cahill, Holger, 99n.
Canary in a Cathouse, 102.
Casey, John, 21n, 57n.
Catch-22, 22, 53.
Cat's Cradle, 6, 10, 12-15, 18, 21n, 23, 26, 30-31, 35, 42, 44-49, 54, 56,
    58n, 67, 74, 80, 88n, 89-90, 93-94, 98n, 102-103; apocalypse, 44-
    49, 89-90; Bokonon, 18, 35, 45, 47-49, 67, 80, 83, 93-94; Bokonon's
    calypsos, 35, 48; Bokonon Creation Myth, 15; Bokonon's view of
    history, 13, 80; Bokonon and Lionel Boyd Johnson, 47; *Books of
    Bokonon*, 23, 45, 49;
comedy, 44-45, 48-49; Langmuir, Irving, 47; model for Felix
Hoenikker, 47; McCabe, Corporal Eugene, 47; narrator, 26, 48-49, 54;
    Mona, 26, 88n.; style, 49.
Celine, Ferdinand, 23, 27, 29.
Chemistry Professor, The, 57n.
Children's Crusade, The, 28.
Chipp, Herchel B., 99n, 100n.
Churchill, Winston, 59.
Class, 87n.
Collier's, 101-102.
concentration camps: *See* death camps.
A Connecticut Yankee in King Arthur's Court, 13.
Cosmopolitan, 102.
courtesy, 81.

"D.P.," 107, 108.
Darwin, Charles, 90.
Deadeye Dick, 6, 9, 17-18, 26, 72, 74, 81-86, 90, 102, 109n, atomic
    bomb, 86; "Bartleby, the Scrivener," and, 83, 88n; the Dark Ages,
    85-86; Job, 82, 83, 88n; murder, 74; neuter, 82, 102; neutron
    bomb, 84, 85, 90; playlets, use of, 82-83, 109n; progress, belief in,
    85; recipes, 83-84; scat singing, 83.

death camps, 56, 107-108.

"Deer in the Works," 98n, 103.

Depression, the Great American, 6-7, 10, 49-50, 54, 77, 97, 99n, 101.

Diogenes, 23, 61n.

Disney, John, 9, 17.

Dresden, 7-8, 14-15, 22-23, 25-26, 28-30, 43, 52-53, 55, 81, 88n; civilian massacre, 14, 22-23, 25-26, 28-29, 43, 81; firebombing, 22, 52-53, 55; footnote to history, 29, 81; Vonnegut as prisoner of war, 23.

Eichmann, Rudolph, 41.

Einstein, Albert, 75-76.

"EPICAC," 104.

Esquire, 21n.

"The Euphio Question," 106.

Figler, John, 88n.

Fitzgerald, F. Scott, 66, 102.

"Flowers on the Wall," 60.

Forever, 30n.

Forgotten Life, 88n.

Fortitude, 57n.

"The Foster Portfolio," 105.

Frankenstein, 41, 57n, 81.

Fussell, Paul, 87n.

Galápagos, 6, 11, 17-20, 50, 70, 77, 89-94, 98n, 102, 103; destruction of the environment, 89-93, 98n; far future as metaphor, 89; narrator, 90-93, 99n; near future, 89; satire, 91-94; style of, 90-93. *See also* Trout, Leon.

Gaule, Charles De, 59.

General Electric, 31-32; Research Laboratory, 47, 101.

Giannone, Richard, 11, 38, 58n, 72, 73n.

"Go Back to Your Precious Wife and Son," 105.

God Bless You, Mr. Rosewater, 6, 12, 14, 23-25, 31, 34, 49-56, 78, 87n, 102, 103, 104; Depression, the Great American, 49-50, 54; Mushari, Norman, 52-53, 55; Rosewater, the model for, 58n; Volunteer Fire Department, 51; World War II, 49, 52-53. *See also* Depression, the Great American and World War II.

Golden Ass, The, 12-13.
Gottlieb, Adolph, 97, 99n.
Goulding, Ray, 59, 87n.
Grapes of Wrath, The, 30n.
Great Gatsby, The, 17, 66.
Gunn, James, 17.
Gussow, Mel, 72n.

Hapgood, Powers, 54, 87n.
Happy Birthday, Wanda June, 6, 9, 59, 72, 72n. *See also* Barnes, Clive; Gussow, Mel.
"Harrison Bergeron," 105.
Harvard, 60.
Heller, Joseph, 22, 53.
Helmholtz, George, 106, 108.
Hickel, Wally, 87n.
Hiroshima, 15, 48.
Hitler, 15, 40, 84.
Holocaust, 14.
Horace, 11-12.
Huckleberry Finn, 13, 21n, 30n.
Hume, Katherine, 58n, 86n, 87n.
Huxley, Aldous, 31.

The Iceman Cometh, 45.
Indianapolis, 5-10, 55; birthplace of Vonnegut, 6.

Jackson, Rosemary, 57n.
Jailbird, 6, 12, 17-19, 50, 54, 65, 68, 72, 74-81, 84, 86, 89, 107-108; "a book . . .for tears!" 79; courtesy in, 81; idealism, 79-80; O'Looney, Mary Kathleen, 74-79, as Mrs. Jack Graham, 76, as shopping bag lady, 76, 77, economic revolution, 78, fairy godmother, 76, fantastic character, 76, illustrates Fussell's theory of American class structure, 87n, poor model of adult behavior, 78-79; prothonotary warblers, 74; RAMJAC Corporation, THE, 74-79; shopping bag ladies, 77-79, nightly rituals, 77-78, produced accidentally, 78; Starbuck, Walter J., 74-81, 87n, model for, 53, 87n, recidivist, 74, 79, Vice President of Down Home Records Division of RAMJAC, 74, 76-77; Trout, Kilgore, 79-80 (Bob Fender, pen name), 75, 79, convicted of treason, 75, fantastic character, 75, harbors spy, 75; the planet Vicuna, 75, "Asleep at the Switch," 75-76. *See also* Hickel, Wally; Nixon, Richard Milhous; Watergate.

"Modest Proposal, A," 40.
Moore, Henry, 95.
"More Stately Mansions," 105-106.
Mother Night, 6-7, 13-15, 19, 21n, 23, 39-44, 47, 54, 56, 57n, 79, 86n, 103; Campbell, Howard, 13, 39-44, 54; collaboration with evil, 13, 23, 39-44; schizophrenia, 41-43, 47, 56, 79; Wertanen, Frank, 40.

National Rifle Association, 85, 88n.
nature, 25.
Nazis, 14, 39-40, 43, 107.
Neibuhr, Reinhold, 16.
"Next Door," 105.
Nichols, Peter, 94.
Nixon, Richard Milhous, 68, 77-81, 87n; American isolato, 80; attitude towards the poor, 77; Congressional Investigating Committee, 79; corruption under, 81; hatred of the American people, 80; loneliness of, 68; only joke, 80; rewards Walter F. Starbuck, 79; witch hunts, 80. *See also Jailbird*, Watergate.
No Exit, 41.

Of Mice and Men, 30n.
Official History of the Army Air Force in World War Two, 29.
O'Neill, Eugene, 45.

Painted Word, The, 96, 98n.
Palm Sunday, 6, 72; as autobiography, 72.
Paulson, Ronald, 11.
The Picture of Dorian Gray, 41.
The Pilgrim's Progress, 37, 57n.
Playboy, 104.
Player Piano, 5, 11-13, 16-17, 31-35, 44, 54, 56, 87n, 89, 98n, 101, 102, 103, 104; automation, 5, 31-35, 56, 104; comedy, 44; distopia, 56; EPICAC XIV, 33, 104; extrapolation, 31; models for, 31; satire, 31-35.
Pogo, 43.
Poirier, Richard, 56.
Pollock, Jackson, 96.
Pope, Alexander, 11-12.

Slaughterhouse-Five, 6-7, 14-19, 22-31, 34-35, 37, 47, 49, 56, 59-60, 66, 71, 89-90, 94; banned and burned, 27, 30n; epitaph, 27; house of salvation, 29; humor, 29-30; Job. 22-30; Judean-Christian theology, 27; drain on Vonnegut, 29-30; Rosewater, Eliot, 28; Tralfamadoreans, 24, 26, 89-90-94; unmotivated human suffering, 14-16, 27, 30; Wildhack, Montana, 16, 26. *See also* Job.
Statler Brothers, 60.
Steinbeck, John, 30n.
Steinberg, Leo, 99n.
Sterne, Laurence, 99n.
Stevenson, Robert Louis, 41.
Stuart, Francis, 34.
Swift, Jonathan, 12, 40, 64.

Tanner, Tony, 21n, 57n.
Thoreau, Henry David, 95.
Tichborne, Chidiock, 84.
Tocqueville, Alexis de, 10.
"Tom Edison's Shaggy Dog," 106.
"Tomorrow and Tomorrow and Tomorrow," 104-105.
Trillion Year Spree, The, 21, 93, 99n.
Trout, Kilgore, 16, 34, 50, 55, 62-65, 73n, 76-81, 98n; failure of, 50, 64; Nobel Prize in medicine, 28; "Asleep at the Switch," 75-76; "The Planet Gobblers," 16; "2BRO2B," 34, 104.
Trout, Leon, 18, 99n; author of *Galápagos*, 18, 90-91.
Twain, Mark, 13, 21n, 30n, 32, 64; Vonnegut names son Mark, 13.

University of Iowa, 43, 64-65.
"Unready to Wear," 106.

Vanzetti, Bartolomeo, 19, 78, 80-81.
Vietnam, 63-64, 92.
Vonnegut, Alice: Vonnegut's audience, 67.
Vonnegut, Jane Cox, 9.